Why Make Your Own Chocolate?

✓ Customise chocolate to match your personal taste

✓ Stronger, richer flavours than commercially available chocolate

✓ Make your guests delicious treats

✓ Make free-from chocolate for vegans, allergy sufferers and people on low-sugar diets

✓ Fill your kitchen with a luscious, molten-chocolate aroma

✓ Never be without a gift idea again

✓ Enjoy the satisfaction of being able to create the object of one of humanity's greatest obsessions

✓ Produce chocolate at will from your baking cupboard

✓ Enjoy the antioxidant, mineral-rich properties of the cocoa bean

✓ Be at the forefront of the inevitable homemade-chocolate-making craze

✓ Add 'chocolatier' to your résumé

Note from Rosen

I want you to enjoy the best possible chocolate-making experience. If you have any questions, please contact me at rosen.trevithick@gmail.com

First published by Trevithick Press, 2015

With thanks to

Nic Drew

for help, support and never tiring of having a piece of chocolate shoved in his mouth the moment he walked through the door.

Sian Wilson

for being a superb photography assistant, Christmas consultant and enthusiastic chocolate taster.

Further thanks to

David Wailing

Storywork Editing Services

storywork.co.uk

And thanks to the recipe testing team

Ann Crawford

Julie Stacey

Dawn Spiteri

Kath Middleton

Jason Hitchins

Ian Mackintosh

Isobel Mackintosh

Chocolate Making Adventures

Create Your Own Chocolate

Rosen Trevithick

Photography by

Claire Wilson

Live Life Explore

Contents

Introduction

Choosing Your Ingredients 8

Equipment 12

Techniques 14

Your Basic Chocolate

Plain and Simple Dark Chocolate 20

Milk Chocolate 22

White Chocolate 24

Ultimate Chocolate 26

Vegan White Chocolate 28

Vegan 'Milk' Chocolate 29

Chocolate for Diabetics 30

Chocolate-Free Chocolate (Carob) 31

Feature: Making Chocolate From Cocoa Beans **32**

Gourmet Chocolate Bars

Smartie and Strawberry Smash 36

Triple Chocolate...38

Flavoured Chocolate 39

Colourful Miniatures...40

Marbled Chocolate with Cocoa Nibs 42

Honey Milk Bars 44

Date and Walnut Crunch 45

Lavender and Blueberry 46

Peppermint Cream...48

Feature: How to Enjoy Chocolate **50**

Individual Chocolates

Clotted Cream Chocolate Mousse 54

Pistachio Pralines..55

Strawberry Hearts 56

Amaretto Crème with Boozy Cherries 58

Chocolate Truffles 60

Millionaire's Salted Caramel Cups 64

Peanut Butter Cups with Oaty Biscuit 66

Blackberry Fools 67

Candied Orange Peel 69

Dark Chocolate Gingers 70

More Recipe Variations 72

Seasonal and Novelty Chocolate

Christmas-Spiced Chocolate Treats 76

Fondant Eggs 78

Chocolate Fondant Models 79

Chocolate Block Building 80

The Chocolate Cupboard

Roasted Cocoa Nibs 84

Cocoa Liquor 84

Vanilla Chips 85

Caramelised Condensed Milk 85

Food Colourings 86

Peanut Butter 88

Cashew Butter 88

Presentation Boxes 89

Silicone Moulds 90

Appendix

Troubleshooting 92

Tempering Chocolate 96

Chocolate Thickness Chart 97

Conversion Chart 98

Introduction

The memory of finding out that I could make chocolate on my kitchen stove is vivid. I was at a small social gathering when my friend Claire told me the news that would change my life forever.

"You mean I can press a few ingredients together and make a chocolate substitute?"

"No, you can make actual chocolate."

I spent the next five minutes checking that my ears were not deceiving me.

Being a chocoholic, I had looked up making chocolate many times, but had always been led to believe that it was impossible without complex machinery. However, times have changed and the key ingredient – cocoa butter – is readily available online, opening the door to endless possibilities.

I immediately ordered a tub of cocoa butter to mix with the cocoa powder and honey I already had. It really was that simple – three ingredients.

As soon as my cocoa butter arrived, I got to work improvising a recipe. I melted the cocoa butter then stirred in cocoa powder and honey until I reached a flavour that made my taste buds explode. Then I poured it into moulds and waited.

After one agonising hour, the chocolate was ready to eat. And – oh my goodness – it was the best thing I had ever tasted. Sweet, rich, dark and full of flavour – just divine.

It wasn't long before I wanted to branch out. Could I make milk and white chocolate too?

I quickly met a stumbling block – it's difficult to get milk into homemade chocolate. The slightest drop of moisture causes the mixture to seize; it becomes a thick treacle that is impossible to work with. Online recipes suggested using powdered milk. However, I found that milk powder made the mixture gritty. Often, my mixture would separate out, leaving a horrible, tasteless mess.

Six months, five types of milk, one food mixer, one coffee grinder, a big hunk of granite, a terrifyingly sharp scraper and many ruined slabs of chocolate later, I arrived at a milk chocolate that was both smooth and tasty. And the best news: I found it painless to replicate.

White chocolate was even more challenging, but after much trial and error, I managed to create a recipe that was every bit as sweet and creamy as the white chocolate I have grown up loving.

I wanted to share my discoveries – nobody should have to waste one slab of chocolate, let alone six months' worth. And so I decided to write a recipe book.

Coincidentally, Claire was beginning a career in food photography. As the person who inadvertently kick-started my chocolate-making journey, it seemed perfectly fitting for her to take the role of photographer.

In addition to many recipes for pure chocolate, I've packed this book with ideas on how to flavour, present and embellish it.

I recommend starting with Plain and Simple Dark Chocolate (p.20) to get to grips with chocolate making. Once you've mastered that, move on to some of the more complex varieties.

Best of luck with your chocolate-making adventures.

Rosen

Choosing Your Ingredients

Cocoa Extracts

Cocoa Butter

Cocoa butter can relate to two things: the pure, pale yellow, edible fat extracted from cocoa beans, or a skin cream derived from it. Naturally, it's very important to purchase the edible sort, as these are definitely *not* interchangeable. Some people refer to the edible cocoa butter as *cacao* butter, but it's essentially the same thing.

You need to buy cocoa butter, as you can't make it at home without complex machinery.

Cocoa butter is made from cocoa nibs, the brown bits found inside cocoa beans. It's extracted, leaving cocoa solids, which are also used in chocolate making.

Edible cocoa butter is usually sold 'raw'. Controversially, heat is often used in the process of extracting cocoa butter. However, don't get bogged down in debates like 'How raw is raw?' because my recipes will involve raising the temperature to over 45°C anyway.

Cocoa butter is solid at room temperature and takes a while to melt, so I recommend buying it in button or medallion form.

Cocoa butter can be very expensive unless you buy in bulk (bags of 1kg or more). Even so, I recommend buying a small tub or bag to begin with, and progressing to a larger bag once you've got a taste for chocolate making. Alternatively, form a chocolate syndicate with friends.

Cocoa Butter For White Chocolate

Cocoa butter has a strong flavour, which can overpower other ingredients, such as milk. In order to make delicious white chocolate, you will need to select *deodorised* cocoa butter. Be aware that this lacks the nutritional value of unprocessed cocoa butter.

Cocoa Powder

Cocoa powder is made from grinding the solids that remain after cocoa butter has been extracted from the nibs.

I use *roasted* cocoa powder. You can buy raw powder but I found it less flavoursome than its roasted counterpart. I ended up using it for face masks rather than cooking.

As with choosing cocoa butter, bear in mind that my recipes involve temperatures up to 45°C, which exceeds standards on what can be considered raw.

Watch out for additives when you buy roasted cocoa powder. Some supermarkets like to lace theirs with unnecessary extras.

Cocoa Liquor

Also known as cocoa paste, cocoa liquor is a product made from ground cocoa nibs that have been separated from their shells. Usually cocoa liquor is separated into cocoa solids and cocoa butter, but you can buy the liquor itself. It makes delicious, rich and smooth chocolate.

Cocoa liquor tends to be bitter. Some kinds have a smoky taste. However, you only need to add a little sweetener and additional cocoa butter to turn it into dark chocolate.

Most of my recipes use cocoa powder instead of cocoa liquor, but if you want to make chocolate from scratch, you'll need to work with liquor.

Although the name suggests that this product resembles a paste or liquor, at room temperature it's actually the texture of plain chocolate – solid.

SWEETENERS

Dozens of different sweeteners can be used for making chocolate. You may wish to find a sweetener of your own. It depends on your priorities: taste, texture or particular health benefits.

Honey

This is the sweetener I use in most of my chocolate, because it adds depth of flavour as well as sweetness.

Suggestions that honey is healthier than sugar have largely been discredited. However, you can get away with using relatively small quantities, because it's sweeter.

All of the ingredients in chocolate need to be eaten in moderation; honey is no different.

Agave Nectar

Agave comes in liquid form – like a runny syrup – and is very easy to combine with other ingredients. Having a fairly mild taste, it adds sweetness without overpowering other ingredients. Being very much a food of the moment, it's relatively easy to come by.

People first believed agave nectar was a healthy alternative to sugar. It has since been shown that agave is *not* a health food. For example, it contains more calories than sugar. It does, however, have the advantage that it's sweeter, so you can use less.

Agave nectar is vegan and you can substitute honey for agave nectar in any of my recipes.

Sweetened condensed milk

I use condensed milk to sweeten white chocolate.

It has the consistency of runny treacle, and is used to add creaminess to a recipe. This product is full of sugar, meaning that recipes using condensed milk rarely need further sweetening.

It is not healthy, but my goodness, is it tasty.

Sugar

Being finely ground, icing sugar is the best cane sugar for smoothly combining with the other ingredients. However, the flavour lacks the richness of honey, and I find sugar can make chocolate taste a little sickly.

Golden icing sugar is slightly nicer than white, but still not a patch on other sweeteners, in my opinion.

Date Nectar

This is my favourite sweetener. It has a similar consistency to honey and agave nectar but with a rich, dark, treacle-like taste. You can certainly identify dates if you dab a bit on your finger and lick it.

Date nectar should be reserved for recipes where you don't mind the unique flavour of the sweetener taking a dominant role in the finished flavour.

Stevia

Stevia is extracted from plant leaves, and is generally considered a natural and low calorie alternative to sugar. It is available as granules and in liquid form, with liquid stevia being by far the best variety for chocolate making, as it's non-gritty.

The liquid is highly concentrated, which means that you can add a great deal of sweetness without unsettling the texture.

However, although stevia undoubtedly adds sweetness, I've found that the flavour lacks depth and leaves a horrible aftertaste.

Therefore, I recommend using stevia sparingly and only in combination with another sweetener.

MILK AND CREAMS

It's difficult to get milk into chocolate, because water causes it to seize, creating a horrible, syrupy mess that you can't work with. Therefore, you need to use products derived from milk, rather than milk itself.

Full Cream Milk Powder

This is the milk product that I use when making milk chocolate, because it contains no moisture at all. However, it can be difficult to achieve a smooth texture using this powder.

Milk powder can't dissolve in cocoa butter, so the trick is to make the milk powder so fine that your tongue can't detect it. You can improve its texture by whizzing milk powder in a coffee grinder until it reaches the fineness of flour.

Chocolate making requires *full cream* milk powder (also known as 'whole milk'). Skimmed milk powder does not create the desired creaminess or consistency.

Powdered and instant are two different types of milk powder. Powdered milk tends to be very pure, while instant milk powder usually contains an emulsifier such as lecithin. The additives help the milk powder dissolve, but are not necessary, because all my recipes include a step that helps the ingredients combine without chemicals.

Sweetened Condensed Milk

This has the texture of syrup and is made purely from evaporated milk and sugar, thus it appears in both ingredient sections.

Because the water has been evaporated off, condensed milk is much better for chocolate making than actual milk. Sweetened condensed milk is great for giving chocolate a really creamy texture.

As you increase the amount of condensed milk in a recipe, the texture of your finished product becomes more like fudge than chocolate, so use sparingly.

Clotted Cream

Cream can be used to add milk to a recipe, particularly clotted cream which is very thick. You can generally get away with adding a couple of tablespoons per 100g cocoa butter, but too much thins the chocolate, making the finished product more like truffles than chocolate.

Cashew Butter

The consistency of cashew butter, which is literally just ground cashew nuts, is perfect for adding creaminess to chocolate. It's an ideal milk substitute for vegans.

Coconut Butter

Coconut butter is a popular substitute for cocoa butter. It's more readily available, being stocked by most supermarkets and health food shops. Coconut butters vary in flavour, with some tasting rich and tropical, while others taste fairly neutral.

The main disadvantage of coconut butter is that it has a very low melting point. Chocolate containing large quantities of coconut oil melts quickly in the hands.

It's useful to keep a jar of coconut butter in the cupboard, because it is the easiest way to add creaminess to a mixture that tastes too strongly of cocoa powder. Cocoa butter takes a long time to melt, so can be annoying to add at the end, whereas coconut butter dissolves almost instantly.

FLAVOURINGS

Essences and Extracts

Commercially available flavourings are usually made by combining a concentrated form of an ingredient with a carrier, such as alcohol or water. This is a problem for chocolatiers, as a single drop of water can ruin a perfectly decent batch of chocolate.

I've had some success adding watery extracts to homemade chocolate, but it's rather hit and miss, so I recommend using other forms of flavouring where possible.

Oils

Flavoured oils have the advantage that they contain no water.

If you choose to use oils, be sure to get culinary grade products, as many essential oils are sold for aromatherapy and not supposed to be consumed.

Oils are highly concentrated, so use them sparingly. Additionally, too much oil can thin a chocolate, preventing it from setting.

Ingredients Themselves

Some flavours are very easy to create yourself:

- Vanilla flavour can be made by scraping vanilla seeds from a pod straight into molten chocolate.
- Coconut flavour can be made by substituting half of the cocoa butter with a good quality coconut butter.
- Cinnamon flavour can be made by shaking dry cinnamon powder into a chocolate mixture.
- Coffee flavour can be made by adding espresso powder to a chocolate mixture.

Some ingredients, such as cranberries, dried lime and chilli pieces, can be embedded in the chocolate itself, giving brief hits of flavour amongst an otherwise simple bar of chocolate.

Another way to add flavour to chocolate is to use soft centres. Fresh strawberry juice, for example, isn't suitable for flavouring chocolate itself, but makes a delicious cream filling.

COLOURINGS

Chocolate is so naturally appetising that the ingredients speak for themselves. However, occasionally a recipe calls for a touch of colour, for example to distinguish similar chocolates or to make decorations.

I often use homemade colours (p.86) because although artificial additives provide the most vibrant colours, I prefer to cook with natural ingredients.

You can buy both natural and artificial colours from the supermarket but these additives often contain water and alcohol, which can cause chocolate to seize.

OTHER ADDITIVES

Why No Lecithin?

Lecithin is an additive that can be used to thicken chocolate and help prevent the ingredients from separating. There has been speculation about potential dangers but very little evidence to back up concerns.

Nevertheless, the controversy does make it somewhat unappealing. With a little patience, ingredients can be combined on a slab without any need for an emulsifier. Thus, I've avoided using lecithin in my recipes.

Equipment

MELTING POT

The best way to melt chocolate is to put it in a basin above boiling water. This ensures that the chocolate is exposed to a steady flow of heat and doesn't get too hot. You can easily balance a heatproof bowl on top of a saucepan, but depending on the exact nature of your equipment, removing the bowl from the heat might be a little fiddly. If you're going to be making a lot of chocolate, you might want to consider buying a designated melting pot. I use a stainless steel pot with a slight spout, which makes it easy to pour.

No Suitable Saucepan?

Fill one bowl with boiling water and rest another on top of it. You may need to replace the water every so often to keep it hot.

CHOCOLATE MOULDS

The easiest moulds to use are made of silicone; these are flexible and allow you to easily pop the chocolate out once it's set.

The type of mould to use depends on what you want to make. If you want to wow people with simple, unadulterated chocolate, you can't beat a traditional bar mould.

Chocolates made in individual moulds make great presents. To really impress people, buy three or four moulds in different shapes.

If you are going to fill your chocolate, make sure that the moulds are fairly deep – at least 15mm.

If you have a choice of colours, go for something that will contrast with chocolate so that you can easily see which sides have already been covered. Annoyingly, most moulds are sold in brown.

No Moulds?

Try plastic cups, yoghurt pots or silicone bun cases.

GRANITE / MARBLE SLAB

Polished granite and marble slabs are used to quickly cool and work chocolate (see p.14).

I use this technique to combine ingredients that don't want to mix readily, for example cocoa butter and condensed milk; as they cool, they bind together. You can also use a slab to temper chocolate (p.96).

Try not to use your slab as a general worktop saver. Knives and other sharp kitchen utensils can ruin their polished surfaces.

A 400 x 300mm slab is ideal for the quantities of chocolate used in this book.

No Slab?

You can use a chopping board for this, but make sure that it has a smooth surface.

Some people have used baking trays. If you choose this method, make sure you use the biggest tray you can find, so you can really increase the surface area of the chocolate. Refrigerating the tray beforehand will help the chocolate to thicken quickly.

Avoid working chocolate on your worktop, as the tools could scratch the surface.

SCRAPER AND PALETTE KNIFE

When working chocolate on a slab, you need tools to work the chocolate and stop it running off the sides. You can do this with just one tool – a palette knife or a scraper – but I've found it easier to work with two, and use one to scrape chocolate off the other.

A chocolate scraper looks very much like the sort of hand scraper you use in DIY. If you can't find an affordable chocolate scraper, I see no reason not to use a DIY scraper instead, provided it has an even edge.

A kitchen palette knife is a flat, blunt-edged kitchen tool traditionally used to spread icing. Not to be confused with an artist's palette knife, which is used primarily for painting.

No Scraper?

Try using the blunt edge of a spatula.

DIPPING TOOLS

You can coat sweets in chocolate using a fork or pair of forks. However, it's a tad fiddly.

If you're planning to do lots of coating, you may wish to consider getting specialist tools for the job.

Dipping tools are delicate shapes with handles: some are little spiral cradles, others are fine forks, some are basket-like.

They do make it easy to coat items without either dropping them in the mixture or leaving a massive fork print on them.

PRESENTATION BOXES

Once you've learnt to make homemade chocolate, you will want to give it to everybody and anybody that you care about. You'll quickly find that your Tupperware ends up distributed all over the neighbourhood, or that you're looking for something more visually pleasing than an old ice cream tub. One way to get around this is to use dedicated, cardboard presentation boxes.

Buying Boxes

The boxes you need will probably be much smaller than you think. Shop-bought chocolates are generally served in moulded plastic trays, which deliberately spread out the chocolate. Unless you're going to devote time to making inserts, your chocolates will be presented close together.

Flat-packed boxes for mailing slices of wedding cake are ideal for packaging 8-10 individual sweets.

Making Boxes

On page 89, I teach you how to make your own presentation boxes using just card and scissors; you won't even need glue or sticky tape.

You can vary the dimensions to suit the chocolate that you are trying to package.

Lining Boxes

Not all cardboard is suitable for food use. I was quite horrified when a stack of mail-ordered, flat-packed boxes turned up unwrapped.

I suggest lining your boxes. You could use patterned greaseproof paper or confectioner's foil. Beware of tissue paper – the dye can come out.

Patterned greaseproof paper can also be used to separate layers of chocolate.

Techniques

Each recipe contains basic instructions. However, in some cases you might wish to delve further into the techniques used. This section provides more detailed information.

MEASURING SPOONFULS

Unless otherwise stated, a spoon mentioned in my recipes refers to a level spoonful. A tablespoon (tbsp) is the equivalent of 3 teaspoons (tsps). You can use your regular cutlery for measuring spoonfuls; they're usually, but not always, accurate. If you're concerned about accuracy, you should invest in some dedicated measuring spoons.

MELTING COCOA BUTTER

Cocoa butter melts slowly. You can speed up the process by using small pieces, such as drops or buttons. If your cocoa butter came as chunks, chop or grate it into smaller pieces before melting.

Never melt cocoa butter in a pan directly as the heat will be too strong. Always melt it in a heatproof container over boiling/boiled water. It's best if the container doesn't touch the water.

When following my recipes, you don't want the cocoa butter to get much above 45°C because the hotter it gets, the longer it will take to cool on a slab – an essential stage that must be completed before you can mould your chocolate. The best way to stop the cocoa butter getting too hot is to take it off the heat as soon as the last drops of cocoa butter have melted.

COOLING CHOCOLATE ON A SLAB

You will notice that many of my recipes tell you to pour molten chocolate onto a slab and 'work it'. There are two reasons for this:

1. Some ingredients only combine when the chocolate starts to cool.
2. As it cools, cocoa butter can form six different types of crystal. Only one of these is desirable for smooth, shiny chocolate that makes a satisfying snap when broken. Quickly cooling chocolate then re-heating it allows only this one type of crystal to survive.

The best surface to use is a slab (p.12). Use tools such as a scraper (p.13) to spread the chocolate as thin as possible (less than 1mm deep). This increases the surface area and helps it to cool. Scrape the chocolate back together and repeat. Working the chocolate vigorously, especially as it starts to solidify, will result in a smoother, 'snappier' chocolate.

Some chocolates, like plain and vegan, will take a while to thicken. Others, for example milk and white, will thicken quickly due to the quantities of additional ingredients.

You should aim to scrape the chocolate back into its bowl once both of two conditions have been met:

1. The ingredients have combined smoothly.
2. Your ingredients have reached the consistency of margarine.

It may be hard to catch chocolate at the 'margarine' stage and you may find its texture becomes more solid. Do not worry, just scrape it back into the bowl as quickly as you can and continue with your recipe.

Add additional ingredients to your melted cocoa butter.

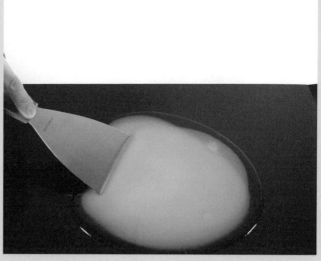

Transfer to a slab.

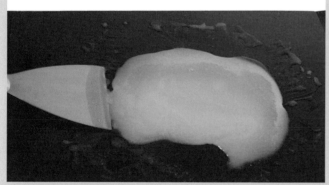

Work the chocolate using a scraper.

As it cools, the chocolate will start to combine smoothly.

Return the chocolate to the heat.

Gently heat and stir until thin enough to pour.

MEASURING THE TEMPERATURE OF CHOCOLATE

I've avoided mentioning temperatures in most of my recipes in order to make them more accessible and because, with ingredient proportions varying from reader to reader, the critical temperatures are hard to predict.

If you do decide to use a thermometer, bear in mind that many kitchen thermometers can be slow to take a reading, by which time your chocolate may be ruined. If you wish to use a thermometer, choose one designed for chocolate. Make sure it doesn't touch the base of your bowl.

CHECKING THAT CHOCOLATE WILL SET

You've just made a batch of chocolate and you're ready to pour it into moulds, but you want to be sure that it'll set properly first. This is particularly useful if you're making chocolates to fill.

Dip a teaspoon into the molten chocolate and pop it in the fridge for 5 minutes. If the chocolate comes out set, then your mixture is perfect. If it doesn't, then consider returning the chocolate to the slab and repeating the cooling/reheating process.

ADAPTING RECIPES

I've provided a range of different techniques, from which you can choose your favourites. For example, you can add milk to chocolate in either powdered or condensed form. I have described both methods. You'll find powdered milk in my milk chocolate and condensed in my white. However, there's no reason not to make milk chocolate with condensed milk or white chocolate with powdered milk. It all depends on your priorities. Chocolate made with condensed milk is smoother than chocolate made with milk powder, but it's not as solid.

Each recipe can be customised to make your personal favourite chocolate. For example, you can increase honey for a sweeter chocolate, or increase cocoa powder for a richer chocolate. Just make sure that you don't exceed the maximum quantities of honey and milk, or your chocolate will not set.

STORING CHOCOLATE

Homemade chocolate is generally best kept in the fridge. Some kinds, such as dark, will be fine in a cool, dark cupboard, provided the slab stage was completed successfully. However, chocolate containing milk can go off if not kept chilled. Any chocolate containing coconut butter must be kept in the fridge, as it has a very low melting point.

You can keep most simple chocolate for up to 5 days, provided that its ingredients, such as sweetened condensed milk, were freshly opened. If you're not sure, refer to your specific recipe. It is likely that this is a very conservative estimate. While some cans of condensed milk say you must consume within 5 days of opening, plenty of sources state that you can keep it for longer.

Some chocolate fillings greatly diminish the shelf life of chocolate, such as those that use clotted cream. Make sure you eat clotted cream chocolate within 3 days of making it, and before the use-by date on the cream.

In all honesty, it's unlikely the chocolate will last more than 48 hours before being guzzled.

Crisp, candy shells sometimes discolour if kept in the fridge, as they attract moisture. It's best to create Smartie and Strawberry Smash just before you're ready to eat or present it.

USING SHOP-BOUGHT CHOCOLATE

My recipes assume that you're making your own chocolate but many, for example filled chocolates, can be easily made with shop-bought chocolate.

Couverture chocolate is a high-quality chocolate that contains extra cocoa butter, making it ideal for reworking. However, it is expensive and needs to be tempered in order to achieve a smooth finish and satisfying texture.

The best readily available chocolate for melting is supermarkets' own-brand budget chocolate. Some of the mainstream, brand-named chocolate, especially those that boast creaminess, do not melt well. You might not get a perfect finish with budget chocolate, but you'll create a very respectable and perfectly tasty approximation.

Simply break your chocolate into squares and heat it in a melting pot above a pan of boiling water. If applicable, temper as directed by the manufacturer. Then use as though you made it yourself.

A NOTE ON CLIMATE

These recipes were developed in Cornwall, England, throughout the year. People living in warmer climates may find it harder to make chocolate at home, especially in summer. My advice is to get your kitchen as cool as possible beforehand. Cooler climates should not be a problem, provided that you don't live in an igloo.

Your Basic Chocolate

The recipes in this section serve two purposes: creating mouth-watering bars of chocolate that are delicious in their own right, and making chocolate that can be complemented by other ingredients in later recipes.

The methods may seem alien to you at first, with counter-intuitive lowering and raising of the chocolate temperature, but bear with it. It takes a while to get a feel for the chocolate-making process. Once you've got the knack, you'll soon be making chocolate for every occasion.

If you do encounter problems, I've included a comprehensive troubleshooting section at the back of the book. You *will* nail this.

I've catered for people with a variety of dietary requirements, including vegan, low-sugar diets, and even chocolate allergies.

Right: vegan white, carob and diabetic chocolate

Plain and Simple Dark Chocolate

You will need chocolate moulds, yoghurt pots or plastic cups.

INGREDIENTS

60g cocoa butter

up to 4 tsp honey

up to 5 tsp cocoa powder

1 vanilla chip (optional) (p.85)

✔ vegan (use agave instead of honey)

✔ nut free

✔ gluten free

makes roughly 100g

(e.g. two 80 x 100 x 9mm bars)

METHOD

1. Start with a cool, dry kitchen.

2. Place the cocoa butter and vanilla chip in a heatproof bowl above a pan of boiling water. Stir from time to time, until melted. This usually takes 5-6 minutes. Remove from the heat.

3. Add half of the honey and stir.

4. Add half of the cocoa powder, continuing to stir. Taste the mixture. If it is too bitter, add honey, ½ tsp at a time, to taste. If it's not chocolatey enough, add cocoa powder little by little.

5. Being careful to wipe any condensation off the bottom of the bowl, pour the mixture onto a slab, using a scraper and/or palette knife to ensure that it doesn't run off the edges.

6. Cool the mixture by working it back and forth with the scraper. Repeatedly spread it out to increase the surface area then scrape it back together. If the mixture doesn't start to thicken after 5 minutes, try opening a window to cool down your kitchen.

7. Once the mixture resembles the consistency of margarine, scrape it back into the bowl and return it to the pan. You should not need to return the water to the boil as a gentle heat will suffice.

8. Stir until the chocolate is *just* thin enough to pour or leave slightly thicker if you're going to use it for coating/filling (see Chocolate Thickness Chart p.97). Allowing the chocolate to become too thin could cause the ingredients to separate in the mould.

9. To make a chocolate bar, place a silicone chocolate mould on a solid object such as a placemat or chopping board, so that you can lift it without spilling the chocolate.

10. Pour the molten chocolate into your moulds.

11. Immediately transfer the chocolate to the fridge to set.

12. After 1 hour, remove the moulds from the fridge and carefully pop out the chocolate.

13. If any remains uneaten after the first hour, store in a cool, dry place for up to 5 days.

Milk Chocolate

When people think of milk chocolate, they tend to think of a very specific blend of milk, cocoa and sugar. It's usually mid-brown and categorically different from its cousins: white and plain. In actual fact, milk chocolate is on a spectrum, with the taste and colour affected by both milk and cocoa powder. Use too much cocoa powder and you'll hardly taste the milk.

In this recipe, I've reduced the quantity of cocoa powder used in my plain chocolate, to bring out the milky flavour. Feel free to experiment with the proportions, to your own taste. If you find the cocoa overpowers the milk, you could try using *deodorised* cocoa butter instead of regular.

You will need chocolate moulds, yoghurt pots or plastic cups.

INGREDIENTS

55g cocoa butter

up to 5 tsp honey

up to 1 tbsp cocoa powder

2 tbsp full cream powdered milk

1 vanilla chip (p.85)

✔ vegetarian

✔ nut free

✔ gluten free

makes roughly 100g

(e.g. two 80 x 100 x 9mm bars)

METHOD

1. Start with a cool, dry kitchen.

2. Place the cocoa butter and vanilla chip in a heatproof bowl above a pan of boiling water. Stir from time to time, until melted. This usually takes 5-6 minutes. Remove from the heat.

3. Add half the honey and half the cocoa powder, then stir.

4. Milk powder won't dissolve into cocoa butter, so the trick is to make the powder so fine that the tongue cannot detect the grains. If your milk powder already has the consistency of flour, you can use it 'as is'. If not, put it in a coffee grinder for 3-4 minutes, or until perfectly smooth.

5. Stir the milk powder into the rest of the mixture.

6. Being careful to wipe any condensation off the bottom of the bowl, pour the mixture onto a slab, using a scraper and/or palette knife to ensure that it doesn't run off the edges.

7. Cool the mixture by working it back and forth with the scraper. Repeatedly spread it out to increase the surface area then scrape it back together. If the mixture doesn't start to thicken after 5 minutes, try opening a window to cool down your kitchen.

8. Taste your mixture. If it's not chocolatey enough, add cocoa powder, little by little. If it's not sweet enough, add a little more honey, continuing to mix with your scraper.

9. If you're happy with the flavour, then once the ingredients have combined smoothly and reached the texture of margarine, scrape it back into the bowl and return to the pan.

10. Stir until the chocolate is just thin enough to pour, or slightly thicker if you're going to use it for coating/filling (see Chocolate Thickness Chart p.97). Allowing the chocolate to become too thin could cause the ingredients to separate in the mould.

11. Pour into moulds and transfer to the fridge immediately. Allow to set for 1 hour, or use as directed in your recipe. Store for up to 5 days in the fridge.

White Chocolate

There's a trick to creating the perfect white chocolate, and that's **deodorised** cocoa butter. The rich flavour of regular cocoa butter overpowers milk and sugar, which are the main flavours people like to detect when enjoying white chocolate. If you use the recommended cocoa butter, then the resulting chocolate will be sweet, creamy and delicious – the perfect contrast to plain.

You will need chocolate moulds, yoghurt pots or plastic cups.

INGREDIENTS

60g **deodorised** cocoa butter

2 tbsp sweetened condensed milk

1 tbsp full cream powdered milk (optional)

1 vanilla chip (p.85)

✔ vegetarian

✔ nut free

✔ gluten free

makes just over 100g

(e.g. two 80 x 100 x 9mm bars)

METHOD

1. Start with a cool, dry kitchen.

2. Place the cocoa butter and vanilla chip in a heatproof bowl above a pan of boiling water. Stir from time to time, until melted. This usually takes 5-6 minutes. Remove from the heat.

3. In a small cup, dissolve the powdered milk into the condensed milk. This thickens the condensed milk and helps get more milk into the chocolate. However, don't worry if you don't have milk powder, the chocolate will be delicious and creamy with the condensed milk alone.

4. Spoon the milk mixture into the molten cocoa and stir. The mixture is likely to look a horrible mess and you may wonder if it will ever combine – trust me, it will during the next steps.

5. Being careful to wipe any condensation off the bottom of the bowl, pour the mixture onto a slab, using a scraper and/or palette knife to ensure that it doesn't run off the edges.

6. Cool the mixture by working it back and forth with the scraper. Repeatedly spread it out to increase the surface area then scrape it back together. If the mixture doesn't start to thicken after 5 minutes, try opening a window to cool down your kitchen.

7. If you're happy with the flavour, then once the ingredients have combined smoothly and reached the texture of margarine, scrape it back into the bowl and return to the pan. You shouldn't need to return the water to the boil; a gentle heat will suffice.

8. Stir until the chocolate is just thin enough to pour, or slightly thicker if you're going to use it for coating/filling (see Chocolate Thickness Chart p.97). Allowing the chocolate to become too thin could cause the ingredients to separate in the mould.

9. Pour into moulds or use as directed in your recipe.

10. Immediately transfer the chocolate to the fridge to set.

11. After 1 hour, remove the moulds from the fridge and carefully pop out the chocolate.

12. Store in the fridge for up to 5 days.

Ultimate Chocolate

Most of my chocolate uses cocoa powder, because most people have it in their baking cupboards already. However, cocoa liquor is less processed than powder, thus results in a more palate-smacking chocolate, especially if you make your own liquor (p.84). I like to balance the intense, smoky flavour of the liquor with creamy condensed milk.

You will need chocolate moulds, yoghurt pots or plastic cups.

INGREDIENTS

40g cocoa butter

Up to 30g cocoa liquor (p.84)

2 tbsp sweetened condensed milk

1 vanilla chip (optional) (p.85)

✔ vegetarian

✔ nut free

✔ gluten free

makes roughly 100g

(e.g. three 45 x 110 x 10mm bars)

METHOD

1. Start with a cool, dry kitchen.

2. Place the cocoa butter, half the liquor and a vanilla chip in a heatproof bowl above a pan of boiling water. Stir from time to time, until melted. This usually takes 5-6 minutes. Remove from the heat.

3. Stir in the condensed milk. The mixture is likely to look a horrible mess and you may wonder if it will ever combine – trust me, it will during the next steps.

4. Being careful to wipe condensation off the bottom of your melting pot, pour the mixture onto a slab, using a scraper and/or palette knife to ensure that it doesn't run off the edges.

5. Pop the remaining liquor into your melting pot (no need to clean it). Leave it over the heat.

6. Cool the mixture by working it back and forth with the scraper. Repeatedly spread it out to increase the surface area then scrape it back together. If the mixture doesn't start to thicken after 5 minutes, try opening a window to cool down your kitchen.

7. Taste the mixture. If it's not chocolatey enough, add melted liquor little by little and combine, until the mixture is to your taste. This step is required because cocoa liquors vary in strength.

8. Once the ingredients have combined smoothly, reached the consistency of margarine, and you are happy with the taste, scrape the mixture back into the bowl and return to the pan. You should not need to return the water to the boil as a gentle heat will suffice.

9. Stir until the chocolate is just thin enough to pour, or slightly thicker if you're going to use it for coating/filling (see Chocolate Thickness Chart p.97).

10. To make a chocolate bar, place your silicone chocolate mould on a solid object such as a placemat or chopping board, so that you can lift it without spilling the chocolate.

11. Pour the molten chocolate into your mould and immediately transfer to the fridge to set.

12. After 1 hour, remove the chocolate from the fridge and carefully pop it out of the moulds.

13. Store in the fridge for up to 5 days.

Vegan White Chocolate

The combination of coconut butter and cashew butter give this vegan chocolate a sweet, creamy texture similar to traditional white chocolate. Far from being a consolation prize for those who avoid dairy, this chocolate is a perfectly delicious treat in its own right.

You will need chocolate moulds, yoghurt pots or plastic cups.

INGREDIENTS

55g cocoa butter

½ tbsp cashew butter (p.88)

4 tsp agave nectar

2 tsp coconut butter

2 vanilla chips (optional) (p.85)

✔ vegan

! contains nuts

✔ gluten free

makes roughly 100g

(e.g. one 60 x 86 x 20mm bar)

METHOD

1. Start with a cool, dry kitchen.

2. Place the cocoa butter and vanilla chips in a heatproof bowl above a pan of boiling water. Stir from time to time, until melted. This usually takes 5-6 minutes. Remove from the heat.

3. Stir in the cashew butter, coconut butter and agave nectar. The coconut butter will take a few moments to dissolve, but has a low melting point, so should blend in quite quickly. The mixture is likely to look a horrible mess and you may wonder if it will ever combine – trust me, it will during the next steps.

4. Being careful to wipe condensation off the bottom of your melting pot, pour the mixture onto a cool slab, using a scraper and/or palette knife to ensure that it doesn't run off the edges.

5. Work the mixture back and forth until it just starts to thicken. This may take a while. You can speed things along by opening a window to cool down your kitchen.

6. Once the mixture has combined smoothly and reached the texture of margarine, scrape it back into the bowl and return to the pan. You should not need to return the water to the boil as a gentle heat will suffice.

7. Stir until the chocolate is just thin enough to pour, or slightly thicker if you're going to use it for coating/filling (see Chocolate Thickness Chart p.97). Allowing the chocolate to become too thin could cause the ingredients to separate in the mould.

8. Pour into moulds and refrigerate immediately, or use as directed in your recipe.

9. After 1 hour, pop the chocolate out of your moulds.

10. Chocolate containing coconut butter needs to be kept in the fridge. Store for up to 5 days.

For photo, see page 19

Vegan 'Milk' Chocolate

I enjoyed my vegan white chocolate recipe so much that I decided to apply the same technique to create a creamy chocolate that's a happy medium between plain and white. Why should people who drink cow's milk have all the fun?

You will need chocolate moulds, yoghurt pots or plastic cups.

INGREDIENTS

45g cocoa butter

2 tsp cashew butter (p.88)

2 tbsp agave nectar

2 tsp coconut butter

4 tsp cocoa powder

✔ vegan

! contains nuts

✔ gluten free

makes roughly 100g

(e.g. one 60 x 86 x 20mm bar)

METHOD

1. Start with a cool, dry kitchen.

2. Place the cocoa butter in a heatproof bowl above a pan of boiling water. Stir from time to time, until melted. This usually takes 5-6 minutes. Remove from the heat.

3. Stir in the cashew butter, coconut butter, cocoa powder and agave nectar. The coconut butter will take a few moments to dissolve, but has a low melting point, so should blend in quite quickly. The mixture is likely to look a horrible mess and you may wonder if it will ever combine – trust me, it will during the next steps.

4. Being careful to wipe condensation off the bottom of your melting pot, pour the mixture onto a cool granite or marble slab, using a scraper and palette knife to ensure that it doesn't run off the edges.

5. Cool the mixture by working it back and forth with the scraper. Repeatedly spread it out to increase the surface area then scrape it back together. If the mixture doesn't start to thicken after 5 minutes, try opening a window to cool down your kitchen.

6. Once the mixture has combined smoothly and reached the texture of margarine, scrape it back into the bowl and return to the pan. You should not need to return the water to the boil as a gentle heat will suffice.

7. Stir until the chocolate is just thin enough to pour, or slightly thicker if you're going to use it for coating/filling (see Chocolate Thickness Chart p.97). Allowing the chocolate to become too thin could cause the ingredients to separate in the mould.

8. Pour into moulds and refrigerate immediately, or use as directed in your recipe.

9. After 1 hour, pop the chocolate out of your moulds.

10. Chocolate containing coconut butter needs to be kept in the fridge. Store for up to 5 days.

Chocolate for Diabetics

Diabetics have two options: to cut down on sweet foods or use a substitute sweetener.

Sugar substitutes have been shrouded in controversy, with each one seeming to take a turn in the limelight before being heavily criticised. While some have escaped attack, I've found that many sweeteners, for example stevia, leave a bitter aftertaste in the mouth and have not resulted in chocolate I would like to eat.

Therefore, I recommend that you avoid seeking a wonder sweetener and instead opt for a high quality chocolate, and eat it in very small quantities.

I use honey to sweeten this chocolate. It's not perfect for diabetics but is sweet enough to be needed in smaller quantities than cane sugar. It is also a natural product, so ideal for those who prefer to avoid artificial, heavily processed ingredients.

I include raisins in this chocolate to help diabetics pace intake. While any sugary fruit needs to be eaten in moderation, raisins are undoubtedly better for diabetics than chocolate.

Some studies suggest that small amounts of chocolate can improve health, but only *plain* chocolate and the darker the better. Therefore, I discourage adding milk or fillings. Certainly avoid deodorised cocoa butter, as that lacks the goodness found in less processed cocoa products.

You will need chocolate moulds, yoghurt pots or plastic cups.

INGREDIENTS

100g plain chocolate (p.20)

a small handful of raisins

✔ vegetarian

✔ nut free

✔ gluten free

makes roughly 120g

(e.g. two 80 x 100 x 9mm bars)

METHOD

1. While preparing the chocolate, add the honey ½ tsp at a time, to taste – try to get away with the minimum you can enjoy. Adding extra vanilla can help reduce any bitterness. The chocolate is ready to use as soon as it pours smoothly during the reheating stage.

2. Pour the chocolate into a chocolate bar mould, leaving 1mm to spare.

3. Put the mould in the fridge for 2 minutes.

4. Remove the chocolate from the fridge.

5. Drop one raisin onto the chocolate. If it sinks to the bottom, the chocolate needs to be in the fridge longer. You want the raisins to slightly squidge the surface of the chocolate so that they stick.

6. One by one, press the raisins into the chocolate.

7. Return to the fridge. Store for up to 5 days.

Warning: *Eat any chocolate in moderation and, if diabetic, as part of a medically approved diet.*

For photo see page 19

Chocolate-Free Chocolate (Carob)

Let's face it, you wouldn't have this book if you didn't eat chocolate, but perhaps you have a chocolate-intolerant friend or family member.

A favourite alternative to chocolate is carob. Coming from the pod of a flowering shrub, carob has a sweet yet dark taste and does look very similar to chocolate. Combined with the right ingredients, it makes a popular chocolate substitute.

You will need chocolate moulds, yoghurt pots or plastic cups.

INGREDIENTS

80g coconut butter

2 tsp roasted carob powder

2 tbsp icing sugar

1/2 tsp vanilla seeds or paste

✔ vegan

✔ nut free

✔ gluten free

✔ cocoa free

make roughly 100g

(e.g. one 60 x 86 x 20mm bar)

METHOD

1. Start with a cool, dry kitchen.
2. Place the coconut butter in a melting pot above just-boiled water. Mix with a fork until it has a creamy texture that's easy to stir. Remove from the heat. You don't need to heat it until it's like oil; if the coconut butter gets too thin, you'll have to add a time-consuming extra step.
3. Stir in the icing sugar and carob powder.
4. The mixture should be smooth and pourable, with a syrupy texture.

    If the texture is like butter, then it is too thick. Apply a little heat, stirring continuously.

    If the mixture has the texture of cooking oil, it's too thin. You will need to work it on a slab until it thickens, to prevent the ingredients separating out in the mould.

    Pour the mixture onto a slab, using a scraper and/or palette knife to ensure that it doesn't run off the edges. Work the mixture back and forth until it starts to thicken. This may take a while, as coconut butter has a low melting point. You can take breaks while you get on with other things. If it still won't thicken, open a window to cool down your kitchen.

5. Pour the carob into moulds.
6. Refrigerate immediately.
7. After 1 hour, remove the carob from the fridge and pop it out of the moulds.
8. Carob made with coconut butter needs to be kept in the fridge. Store for up to 5 days.

For photo see p.19

Making Chocolate From Cocoa Beans

This page will familiarise you with the chocolate-making process and enable you to use cocoa beans in any of my plain or milk recipes, should you prefer real beans to processed cocoa powder.

Turning cocoa beans into chocolate is time-consuming. However, it's very satisfying to know you've made chocolate from scratch. Certainly, the intense flavour will reward you for your efforts.

Cocoa Beans

Cocoa beans are dried, fermented seeds that grow from the cacao plant in hot countries such as parts of South America and Africa. Peru, Ecuador and Nigeria are particularly famous for their cocoa beans.

Roasting the Beans

First, you roast the cocoa beans to bring out the flavour. This can be done in an ordinary oven. You remove the shells to leave the nibs (p.84).

Grinding the Nibs

Next, you grind the nibs until they become cocoa liquor (p.84). This substance is solid at room temperature, but the heat from grinding gives it a paste-like texture.

Separating the Cocoa Butter and Cocoa Solids

Factories use a hydraulic press to separate cocoa liquor into yellow cocoa butter and a solid mass called cocoa presscake, which is later cooled, pulverized and sifted to make cocoa powder. Few home kitchens contain a hydraulic press, but it doesn't matter because you can make delicious plain and milk chocolate without separating the cocoa liquor.

The proportions of cocoa butter and cocoa powder used in the tastiest chocolate are not the same as the proportions found naturally in cocoa liquor, therefore you need to add additional cocoa butter.

Sweetening the Chocolate

The only other ingredient necessary to turn this tasty cocoa mix into chocolate is a little sweetener. I prefer honey because it has a rich flavour and is relatively unprocessed, but it works with other sweeteners such as agave nectar or sugar. Most commercial chocolate contains sugar.

If the resulting chocolate is a little dark for your personal taste, add condensed or powdered milk.

Using Cocoa Liquor in Recipes

My ultimate chocolate (p.26) uses cocoa liquor, but you can use it in any recipe that contains both cocoa powder and cocoa butter. I usually use four times as much liquor as powder, in weight. However, the amount of cocoa liquor required varies from recipe to recipe and depends on the beans used. I recommend first substituting cocoa powder with twice its weight in cocoa liquor, then keep adding liquor until you reach your desired darkness.

Gourmet Chocolate Bars

You've mastered making chocolate and now you want to make something even more special. Perhaps you want to incorporate a friend's favourite fruit, or add some peppermint for an after-dinner treat.

These recipes are intended to inspire you. Either follow them as presented or give them your own unique twist.

Chocolate makes a beautiful backdrop for your favourite sweet, nut or dried fruit. See your chocolate as a canvas and paint it with colour, flavour and texture.

Right: date and walnut crunch, triple chocolate and honey milk

Smartie and Strawberry Smash

Chocolate containing generous chunks of a loved one's favourite snack food makes a great present. Embed jellybeans in milk chocolate bars for somebody with a sweet tooth, or wow a citrus lover with chunks of candied orange enveloped in plain chocolate. In this recipe, I've included two of my personal favourite snacks: Smarties and dried strawberry flakes.

You will need one tray of chocolate bar moulds.

INGREDIENTS

100g milk chocolate (p.22)

a small handful of Smarties

a pinch of strawberry flakes

✔ vegan option (p.29)

✔ nut free (unless vegan)

! contains gluten (but you can buy gluten free sugar coated chocolate beans)

makes roughly 120g

(e.g. two 80 x 100 x 9mm bars)

METHOD

1. Prepare the chocolate.
2. Pour the chocolate into bar-shaped moulds.
3. Immediately drop strawberry flakes onto the chocolate. They should sink.
4. Repeat with Smarties. Keep going until the Smarties stop sinking, and there's an attractive layer of Smarties on top.
5. Return to the fridge for 1 hour.
6. Press out of the moulds.
7. You can store these in the fridge for up to 5 days, but the Smarties may discolour when exposed to moisture.
8. Serve Smartie-side up.

ALSO TRY

Yoghurt-coated strawberries with banana chips.

Jellybeans and broken party rings.

Glace cherries and candied coconut.

Maltesers and fudge cubes.

Oreos and white chocolate buttons.

Triple Chocolate

I've always loved combining white and dark chocolate; contrasting the flavours by taking alternating bites allows each chocolate to accentuate the flavour of the other.

Therefore, I decided to include a recipe for not just white and dark, but milk chocolate too, combined in one delicious bar.

Whether you bite down through all the layers at once, or strip them apart to concentrate on each flavour individually, triple chocolate is a wonderful way to showcase a range of chocolates.

Three colours together looks impressive as well as appetising.

You will need one tray of deep chocolate bar moulds.

INGREDIENTS

100g plain chocolate

100g white chocolate

100g milk chocolate

✔ vegetarian

✔ nut free

✔ gluten free

makes 300g

(e.g. three 60 x 86 x 20mm bars)

METHOD

1. First prepare the plain chocolate. Having the highest cocoa butter content, it provides the shiniest finish, which looks great at the top of the bar.

2. The chocolate is ready to use as soon as it pours smoothly during the reheating stage. Don't allow the mixture to thin too much, as the ingredients could separate in the mould.

3. Fill your chocolate bar moulds to one-third full.

4. Refrigerate.

5. Next prepare the white chocolate. White chocolate is best in the centre, because it visually separates the similar-looking plain and milk chocolate layers.

6. Remove your chocolate moulds from the fridge and fill with the white chocolate until two-thirds full.

7. Refrigerate.

8. Prepare the milk chocolate.

9. Remove your chocolate moulds from the fridge and fill the remaining space with the milk chocolate.

10. Put in the fridge for an hour and a half.

11. Remove from the fridge and carefully press the chocolate out of the moulds.

12. Store in the fridge for up to 5 days.

For photo, see p.35

Flavoured Chocolate

Chocolate is not only delicious alone, but also combines beautifully with other flavours. You'll recognise some favourites:

Chocolate Orange

You can add orange flavouring to any kind of chocolate, but usually people choose milk or dark. I prefer milk chocolate because, being milder than plain, it allows the orange flavouring to stand out. Each citrus has its own perfect companion: white complements lemon while lime pieces are divine within dark.

Peppermint Chocolate

A dark, plain chocolate tastes remarkable when its rich notes are combined with a little refreshing mint. Some people prefer mint to flavour the chocolate itself, while others like to add a smooth, contrasting filling.

Strawberry Chocolate

Strawberry flavouring is relatively mild, so I recommend using it to flavour white chocolate or as a sumptuous filling.

Coffee Chocolate

Coffee is a delicious flavour for chocolate. Adding it to milk chocolate makes a great mocha flavour. To make coffee chocolate, use a teaspoon of espresso powder instead of flavoured oil.

However, the real beauty of flavouring chocolate is that you can be as creative as you like, mixing in all sorts of weird and wonderful ingredients. Start by using different oils to flavour the chocolate itself. Later in this book, I will show you other techniques, such as making centres and candying fruit. This will allow you to incorporate any edible flavour that takes your fancy.

You will need chocolate moulds, yoghurt pots or plastic cups.

INGREDIENTS

100g chocolate of your choice

flavoured oil or espresso powder, to taste

✔ vegan option

✔ nut free (unless vegan)

✔ typically gluten free

METHOD

1. Make chocolate as per your chosen recipe. However, just before transferring it to the slab, add 2 drops of the oil.
2. Taste the chocolate.
3. If the flavour is too mild, continue adding the oil, one drop at a time until you're happy with the flavour. Don't add more than 6 drops, or you could jeopardise the texture of the chocolate.
4. Continue as per your chosen chocolate recipe.

Colourful Miniatures

As a general rule, I prefer not to colour chocolate. Additives can change the flavour and, more importantly, people's *perception* of flavour. Studies have shown that people's visual perception of food can dramatically alter their sense of taste – the first bite really is with the eye.

However, in some circumstances, a splash of colour can add a little excitement or be used to distinguish food.

Mint plain chocolate looks just like orange plain chocolate when it's set, which can be a problem if you're creating a selection of miniatures. A great way to mark your chocolates is to spoon a dash of coloured cocoa butter into the mould before adding the chocolate.

Suggested combinations are mint-flavoured plain chocolate with a dash of green, orange milk chocolate with a splash of orange, and strawberry-flavoured white chocolate with a flash of pink.

You will need one tray of miniature chocolate bar moulds.

INGREDIENTS

100g chocolate of your choice

7g cocoa butter

few drops of food colouring (p.86)

✔ vegan options

✔ nut free (unless vegan)

✔ typically gluten free

makes roughly 107g

(e.g. twenty-four 26 x 36 x 4mm miniatures)

METHOD

1. Place the cocoa butter and food colouring in a heatproof bowl above a pan of boiling water, stirring continuously.

2. As soon as the mixture is thin enough to pour, dab a little on a white plate and allow to set. If the colour isn't strong enough, add more food colouring.

3. Being careful to wipe any condensation off the bottom of the bowl, pour the mixture onto a slab, using a scraper and/or palette knife to ensure that it doesn't run off the edges.

4. Cool the mixture by working it back and forth with the scraper until it reaches the consistency of margarine.

5. Dab tiny dots of the mixture into your chocolate moulds using the end of a spoon handle. Make sure that the dots really are tiny, as this garnish isn't particularly tasty.

6. Immediately transfer to the fridge to set. This will only take a couple of minutes.

7. Meanwhile, prepare a batch of chocolate. The chocolate is ready to use as soon as it pours smoothly during the second heating stage.

8. Retrieve the moulds from the fridge and top them up with chocolate.

9. After 1 hour (sooner if the moulds are very thin), remove the chocolate from the fridge and carefully pop it out of the moulds.

10. Store in the fridge for as long as directed by your chocolate recipe.

Marbled Chocolate with Cocoa Nibs

Cocoa nibs are a rare treat – a little burst of intense, unadulterated chocolate. I personally like to make pesto with cocoa nibs but many people find them too bitter without sugar.

This recipe marbles together two types of chocolate sweet enough to complement the cocoa nibs, but not strong enough to overpower their flavour.

You will need one tray of chocolate bar moulds.

INGREDIENTS

100g milk chocolate (p.22)

100g white chocolate (p.24)

a small handful of cocoa nibs

✔ vegetarian

✔ nut free

✔ gluten free

makes 210g

(e.g. four 80 x 100 x 9mm bars)

METHOD

1. Prepare the milk chocolate. It's ready to use when it's at the coating stage (see Chocolate Thickness Chart p.97) **not** the pouring stage, otherwise it will run when you try to drizzle it.

2. Drizzle the milk chocolate across your moulds. You should aim to fill half the volume of the moulds, while leaving patches of the base empty for the white chocolate to show through.

3. Refrigerate the milk chocolate while you prepare the white.

4. Prepare a batch of white chocolate. It's ready to use when it reaches the pouring stage.

5. Remove the moulds from the fridge and fill them to the brim with the white chocolate.

6. Drop a cocoa nib onto the white chocolate. If it sinks completely, refrigerate the chocolate for 2 minutes. You want the nibs to stick, but not disappear.

7. Once you reach the stage where the nibs stick but don't sink, use them to decorate the upper side of the chocolate.

8. Return to the fridge for an hour.

9. Press out of the moulds.

10. Store in the fridge for up to 5 days.

11. Serve nib-side up.

Honey Milk Bars

I discovered honey milk entirely by accident, while trying to develop a milk chocolate recipe. It's a chewy, nougat-like candy made just from honey and powdered milk. Inspired by Toblerone, I like to set tiny pieces in thick chocolate.

Actual nougat takes a long time to make, typically involving eggs, glucose and sugar, but this yummy two-ingredient alternative can be made in less than 10 minutes.

You will need one tray of deep chocolate bar moulds.

INGREDIENTS

100g milk chocolate made with honey

1 tbsp runny honey

3 tbsp full cream milk powder

✔ vegetarian

✔ nut free

✔ gluten free

makes 110g

(e.g. two 4.5 x 11.5 x 14mm bars)

METHOD

1. Make a batch of chocolate, using honey to sweeten.
2. Using **one half** of the chocolate, half-fill your moulds. Leave the remaining molten chocolate over your pan of water. Stir occasionally but don't apply additional heat unless it starts to set.
3. Place the moulds in the fridge while you prepare the honey milk.
4. Heat 1 tablespoon of honey over a pan of boiling water, until thin.
5. Stir in the milk powder, one spoonful at a time.
6. Heat for 5 minutes, stirring occasionally.
7. Place greaseproof paper on a plate.
8. Spread a thin layer of the honey milk mixture on the greaseproof paper.
9. Allow to cool on a surface for 5 minutes, then put it in the fridge.
10. Occupy yourself for 10 minutes. I recommend clearing up your kitchen!
11. Remove the honey milk from the fridge. With a sharp knife, cut it into tiny pieces (2-3mm).
12. Remove the chocolate from the fridge and position tiny bits of honey milk on it, to taste.
13. Check that the remaining chocolate is still thin enough to pour. Give it a stir. If thinning is required, gently re-heat the boiled water and stir.
14. Pour just enough of the remaining chocolate into each mould so that it covers the honey milk. If there is chocolate left afterwards, top up the moulds with the remainder.
15. Refrigerate for 1 hour.
16. Carefully press the chocolates out of the moulds.
17. Store for up to 5 days.

For photo, see p.35

Date and Walnut Crunch

Date and walnut has been a popular combination for decades. Rather than scattering chocolate with pieces of both, I decided to use date nectar to sweeten the chocolate itself, then decorate with walnuts.

You will need one tray of chocolate bar moulds.

INGREDIENTS

100g plain chocolate, made with date nectar instead of honey (p.20)

a small handful of walnut pieces

✔ vegan

! contains nuts

✔ gluten free

makes roughly 110g

(e.g. two 80 x 100 x 9mm bars)

METHOD

1. Prepare the chocolate, being careful to replace the honey with date nectar.
2. Pour the chocolate into bar-shaped moulds.
3. Drop one walnut piece onto the chocolate. If it sinks to the bottom, put the chocolate in the fridge for 2 minutes. Repeat until a walnut sticks but doesn't sink.
4. Decorate the upper side with the remaining walnut pieces.
5. Return to the fridge for an hour.
6. Press out of the moulds.
7. Store in the fridge for up to 5 days.
8. Serve walnut-side up.

ALSO TRY

Date chocolate smothered in coconut – use crystallised coconut instead of walnuts.

Cinnamon and date chocolate – make your chocolate with ½ teaspoon of cinnamon.

Maple and pecan chocolate – make your chocolate with maple syrup and add pecans.

For photo, see p.35

Lavender and Blueberry

Until recently, it had never occurred to me to use lavender in cooking. Then I ate a slice of lavender and blueberry cake, and never looked back. I decided to take the scrumptious flavours of that cake and combine them with the joys of chocolate.

White chocolate is not only mild enough to allow the lavender to thrive, but its creaminess makes a wonderful companion.

You will need one tray of chocolate bar moulds.

INGREDIENTS

100g white chocolate (p.24)

1 heaped tbsp dried blueberries

½ tsp caster sugar

2 drops lavender oil

✔ vegan (if made with vegan white, p.28)

✔ nut free (unless vegan)

✔ gluten free

makes 150g

(e.g. three 80 x 100 x 9mm bars)

METHOD

1. Prepare a batch of white chocolate. The chocolate is ready to use as soon as it pours smoothly during the second heating stage.

2. Pour the chocolate into your moulds, leaving 1mm to spare.

3. In a small bowl, mix a pinch of caster sugar with two drops of culinary lavender oil. The sugar is there to carry the lavender oil, so that it doesn't all get absorbed by one or two blueberries.

4. Put the blueberries in the bowl with the sugar and give them a good shake.

5. Drop one dried blueberry onto the chocolate. If the blueberry sinks to the bottom, the chocolate needs to go in the fridge for 2 minutes. You want the blueberries to slightly squidge the surface of the chocolate, but not sink.

6. Press the blueberries into the chocolate.

7. Put the chocolate back in the fridge for 1 hour.

8. Remove the chocolate from the fridge and carefully press it out of the moulds.

9. Store in the fridge for up to 5 days.

10. Serve blueberry-side up.

Peppermint Cream

Gone are the days when you needed a saucepan and a selection of (slightly) obscure ingredients in order to make fondant. These days you can pick up fondant icing sugar in most supermarkets.

Fondant makes a wonderful filling for chocolates because it's quick to make, easy to work with and can take on a range of flavours. Peppermint creams are my all-time favourite chocolates.

You will need one tray of deep chocolate bar moulds.

INGREDIENTS

100g plain chocolate (p.20)

40g fondant icing sugar

½ tsp peppermint oil or essence

few drops water

✔ vegan (use agave instead of honey)

✔ nut free (unless vegan)

✔ gluten free

Makes roughly 150g

(e.g. two 4.5 x 11.5 x 14mm bars)

METHOD

1. Prepare a batch of plain chocolate.
2. Use one third of the plain chocolate to part-fill your moulds. You should create a 3-5mm layer. Leave the remaining molten chocolate over your pan of water. Stir occasionally but don't apply additional heat unless it starts to set.
3. Place the moulds in the fridge while you prepare the fondant.
4. Using a fork, combine the fondant icing sugar and peppermint oil. Very slowly, add cold tap water, one drop at a time. You're aiming for a consistency that you can shape in your hands, like modelling clay. If the mixture gets too thin and sticky, add more icing sugar.
5. Remove the moulds from the fridge and check that the chocolate has set, by poking it gently with the handle of a teaspoon.
6. Grab a tiny amount of fondant (the exact size will depend on the size of your moulds). Using your fingers, roll the fondant into a blob.
7. Place your blob on top of your chocolate layer in your first individual mould or, for bars, your first square.
8. Press the blob into shape, making sure that the top of the fondant is at least 2mm lower than the top of the moulds, and does not touch the sides.
9. Repeat for every mould or square. For bars of chocolate, it's best to use a separate blob for each square, otherwise the fondant might show through the grooves.
10. Check that the remaining chocolate is still thin enough to pour. Give it a stir. If thinning is required, gently re-heat the boiled water and stir.
11. Pour just enough of the remaining chocolate into each mould so that it covers the fondant blobs. If there is chocolate left afterwards, top up the moulds with the remainder.
12. Refrigerate for 1 hour.
13. Carefully press the chocolates out of the moulds.
14. Store in the fridge for up to 5 days.

How to Enjoy Chocolate

Everybody knows how to enjoy chocolate, right? Yes of course. With its divine flavour and typically high sugar content, it's impossible not to feel a rush of pleasure when you bite into any piece of chocolate.

But what if I told you that you can enjoy your chocolate even more? In fact, you can get ten times the experience yet not ingest a single extra calorie.

The trick is to completely consume yourself within the experience, a technique borrowed from Mindfulness, a fashionable yet very effective meditation-based practice.

Here's how to do it:

1. Steal yourself a moment alone. Got housemates? Send them out to get some chocolate from the shops – then they'll never guess what you're secretly up to.

2. Lock the door. It doesn't matter if your nearest and dearest has to stand out in the rain for ten minutes; this is your moment.

3. Close the curtains. Turn off your mobile. Unplug your landline at its socket.

4. Blow your nose. Take a drink of water and swirl it around your mouth to cleanse your palate.

5. Put your chocolate on your favourite plate. If it's a chocolate bar, use the whole bar. If it's individual chocolates, select one.

6. Find yourself somewhere comfy to lie, such as your bed, sofa, or on the floor, with your head propped up on a pillow.

7. Close your eyes. Pick up the chocolate and bring it to your nose. Inhale deeply, enjoying its aroma.

8. Now, if you've picked a chocolate bar, break off a square, listening to the pleasant 'snap'.

9. Take a piece of chocolate and explore it with your fingers. What is the surface like? What shape is it? Are there any grooves?

10. Once you've finished teasing yourself, take the chocolate to your lips.

11. Lick the chocolate. Or, if it's too cold to melt, take a tiny nibble.

12. Take a moment to reflect on this first taste. Attend to the sensation of the chocolate in your mouth. How does it feel? Can you detect any individual flavours?

13. Now, take a larger bite and allow yourself to focus on the experience once again.

14. As slowly as you can bear, devour the remainder of the chocolate.

15. Once you've finished your chocolate, take a moment to notice how chocolate tasted better than it ever has before.

16. Now that your entire being has been nourished, you're ready to face anything, including all those people you locked on the doorstep in a thunderstorm.

Individual Chocolates

Individual chocolates are great to serve at a party, or neatly arrange in a presentation box for a loved one.

In this section, you'll find my personal spin on familiar favourites, such as truffles and peanut butter cups, alongside recipes that have been inspired by other things in life, such as fruit fools and millionaire's shortbread.

Clotted cream makes an appearance in some of the recipes, adding a touch of Cornwall, naturally.

You'll also find ideas for variations and more ways to incorporate your own favourite foods, turning a dozen recipes into infinite possibilities.

Right: blackberry fools, pistachio pralines, chocolate mousse

Clotted Cream Chocolate Mousse

Being Cornish, I felt it would be a crime to make chocolate mousse with anything other than clotted cream. Fortunately, this local staple is incredibly special, so very little else is needed to create a wonderful chocolate filling.

You will need one tray of individual, fillable moulds.

INGREDIENTS

100g plain chocolate

50g Cornish clotted cream

10g icing sugar

3 tsp roasted cocoa powder

✔ vegetarian

✔ nut free

✔ gluten free

makes roughly 170g

(e.g. sixteen 27 x 18mm rounds)

METHOD

1. Prepare a batch of plain chocolate. It's ready to use once it's thin enough to spoon, but still thick enough to stick to the sides of the moulds (i.e. the gloopy stage, p.97).

2. Little by little, spoon half of the chocolate into the moulds until each one is about one-third full. Use the handle of a teaspoon to spread it around the sides of each cavity. If the chocolate runs off the sides, put the moulds in the fridge for a couple of minutes and then retry spreading.

3. Place the part-filled moulds in the fridge to set. Leave the remaining molten chocolate over your pan of water. Stir occasionally but don't apply additional heat unless it starts to set.

4. In a separate bowl, combine the cocoa powder, icing sugar and clotted cream.

5. Remove the chocolate cups from the fridge. Using a teaspoon, carefully fill each chocolate with mousse, up to 2mm below the total depth of the mould.

6. Pour just enough of the remaining chocolate into each mould so that it covers the mousse. If there is chocolate left afterwards, top up the moulds with the remainder.

7. Refrigerate for 1 hour.

8. Carefully press the chocolates out of the moulds.

9. Store in the fridge for up to 3 days or until the best-before date of the clotted cream.

For photo, see p.53

Pistachio Pralines

Different countries favour different nuts in their pralines. Popular pralines sold in the UK tend to contain hazelnuts, while the French love almonds, and Americans tend to use pecans. You can basically choose whatever nut you like, or abandon nuts entirely and use seeds. I've always found pistachios more luxurious than other nuts, so they're my favourite base for praline.

You will need one tray of individual, fillable moulds.

INGREDIENTS

100g plain or milk chocolate

25g dairy butter

25g icing sugar

60g shelled pistachios

2 tsp cocoa powder

✔ vegetarian

! contains nuts

✔ gluten free

makes 200g

(e.g. sixteen 26 x 18mm fluted rounds)

METHOD

1. Make a batch of the chocolate of your choice. It's ready to use once it's thin enough to spoon, but still thick enough to stick to the sides of the moulds (i.e. the gloopy stage, p.97).

2. Little by little, spoon half of the chocolate into the moulds until each one is about one-third full. Use the handle of a teaspoon to spread the chocolate around the sides of each cavity. If the chocolate runs off the sides, put the moulds in the fridge for a couple of minutes and then retry spreading.

3. Once coated, place the part-filled moulds in the fridge to set. Leave the remaining molten chocolate over your pan of water. Stir occasionally but don't apply additional heat unless it starts to set.

4. Crush the pistachios into small pieces using a pestle and mortar, if available. You can also use a mini-chopper for this. Choose a consistency that suits you – a fine powder for smooth praline, or tiny pieces for a coarser filling.

5. Sift the icing sugar and cocoa powder into a bowl and stir in the butter using a fork.

6. Stir the ground pistachios into the butter mixture.

7. Take the chocolate moulds from the fridge. Using a teaspoon, carefully fill each chocolate to 2mm below the total depth of the mould.

8. Check that the remaining chocolate is still thin enough to pour. Give it a stir. If thinning is required, gently re-heat the boiled water.

9. Pour just enough of the remaining chocolate into each mould so that it covers the praline. If there is chocolate left afterwards, top up the moulds with the remainder.

10. Refrigerate for 1 hour.

11. Carefully press the chocolates out of the moulds.

12. Store in the fridge for up to 5 days.

For photo, see p.53

Strawberry Hearts

I was delighted when I discovered that you can make strawberry fondant using real strawberries. It's not until you make sweets with fresh fruit that you realise what you're missing when you eat artificially flavoured ones.

You will need one tray of heart-shaped, fillable moulds.

INGREDIENTS

100g of chocolate of your choice

60g fondant icing sugar

50g strawberries (about three)

✔ vegan (use agave instead of honey)

✔ nut free (unless vegan)

✔ gluten free

makes a light 200g

(e.g. sixteen 26 x 30 x 16mm hearts)

METHOD

1. Rinse and destalk your strawberries. Pat completely dry. Blend your strawberries to a pulp, either using a blender or a fork.

2. Place the strawberries in a sieve over a bowl, to collect the juice. You may need to encourage it with a spoon, but don't press strawberry seeds through the mesh.

3. Prepare some chocolate. It's ready to use once it's thin enough to spoon, but still thick enough to stick to the sides of the moulds (i.e. the gloopy stage, p.97).

4. Little by little, spoon half of the chocolate into the moulds until each one is about one-third full. Use the handle of a teaspoon to spread it around the sides of each cavity. If the chocolate runs off the sides, put the moulds in the fridge for a couple of minutes then retry spreading.

5. Place the part-filled moulds in the fridge to set. Leave the remaining molten chocolate over your pan of water. Stir occasionally but don't apply additional heat unless it starts to set.

6. Sieve the icing sugar into a bowl. Very slowly, add strawberry juice, a little at a time. You probably won't need it all. You're aiming for a consistency that you can shape in your hands, like modelling clay. If the mixture gets too thin or sticky, add more icing sugar.

7. Remove the moulds from the fridge and check that the chocolate has set, by poking it gently with the handle of a teaspoon.

8. Grab a tiny amount of fondant. Using your fingers, roll the fondant into a sausage and bend in half, so that it roughly resembles a heart.

9. Place your blob on top of your chocolate layer in your first mould. Press the blob into shape, making sure that the top of the fondant is at least 2mm lower than the top of the moulds, and does not touch the sides.

10. Check that the remaining chocolate is still thin enough to pour. Give it a stir. If thinning is required, gently re-heat the boiled water.

11. Pour just enough of the remaining chocolate into each mould, so that it covers the fondant blobs. If there is chocolate left afterwards, top up the moulds with the remainder.

12. Refrigerate for 1 hour.

13. Carefully press the chocolates out of the moulds.

14. Store in the fridge for up to 5 days.

Amaretto Crème with Boozy Cherries

This recipe was inspired by chocolates I bought on the high street. Cherries and the flavour of almonds sound like an unlikely combo, but they really work. The booze adds an indulgent kick.

You will need one tray of individual, fillable moulds.

Allow 24 hours, as the cherries need to be prepared the night before use.

INGREDIENTS

12 dried cherries

10ml Cointreau

100g chocolate

30g butter

25g icing sugar

5g cocoa powder

½ tsp of Amaretto

✔ vegetarian

✔ can be nut free

    contrary to popular belief, many (but not all) brands of Amaretto are made from peach stones not almonds

✔ typically gluten free

makes 16

(e.g. sixteen 30 x 18mm rounds)

METHOD

1. Count out 12 dried cherries and put them in a small bowl. Cover them with Cointreau and leave overnight for the cherries to soak up the liquid.

2. Make a batch of plain chocolate. It's ready to use once it's thin enough to spoon, but still thick enough to stick to the sides of the moulds (i.e. the gloopy stage, p.97).

3. Pour one half of the chocolate into deep moulds, until they're one-third full. Keep retrieving the chocolate from the fridge and tilting the mould so that the chocolate covers the sides. You might want to encourage it with the handle of a teaspoon. The cooler the chocolate, the more it will stick to the sides. Leave the remaining molten chocolate over the pan of water you used to create it. Stir occasionally but don't apply additional heat unless it starts to set.

4. Make the crème by mixing the butter, icing sugar and cocoa powder using a fork. Add the Amaretto.

5. Remove the moulds from the fridge. Add a boozy cherry to each.

6. Spoon or pipe a little of the crème into each cavity, leaving 2mm for the remaining chocolate.

7. Pour just enough of the remaining chocolate into each mould to cover the praline. If there is chocolate left afterwards, top up the moulds with the remainder.

8. Refrigerate for 1 hour.

9. Carefully press the chocolates out of the moulds.

10. Store in the fridge for up to 5 days.

Chocolate Truffles

Truffles are delicious whether they're dark, milk or white. You can also jazz them up with a little flavouring, such as rum, coffee or chilli powder.

Many truffle recipes use double cream, but I prefer to make mine with condensed milk. It's simple and every bit as tasty as truffles that use a wider range of ingredients.

Condensed milk tends to keep longer than cream, extending the lifetime of your truffles.

INGREDIENTS

Dark Chocolate Truffles

For the coating

100g plain chocolate (p.20)

For the centres

40g cocoa butter

4 tbsp sweetened condensed milk

20g cocoa powder

✔ vegetarian

✔ nut free

✔ gluten free

makes 16

Milk Chocolate Truffles

For the coating

100g milk chocolate (p.22)

For the centres

50g cocoa butter

4 tbsp sweetened condensed milk

10g cocoa powder

✔ vegetarian

✔ nut free

✔ gluten free

makes 16

White Chocolate Truffles

For the coating

100g white chocolate (p.24)

For the centres

50g *deodorised* cocoa butter

5 tbsp sweetened condensed milk

1 vanilla chip or 1 tsp of vanilla essence

✔ vegetarian

✔ nut free

✔ gluten free

makes 16

METHOD

1. Melt the cocoa butter.

2. Stir in the condensed milk and, if applicable, cocoa powder and vanilla. At this stage, it is likely that your mixture will look a mess, with the syrupy milk refusing to combine with the molten cocoa butter. However, don't worry – the ingredients will combine as the mixture cools.

3. Pour the mixture onto a granite or marble slab.

4. Use a scraper and/or palette knife to work the mixture back and forth until the ingredients combine smoothly.

5. Scrape the mixture into a bowl and put in the fridge for 5 minutes. Remove from fridge. If the mixture is firm enough to form balls, it's ready to mould. If not, refrigerate for a further 2 minutes, or until the mixture is thick enough to mould into balls with your fingers. Don't leave the mixture in too long or you'll have to re-heat it before you can shape it.

6. Place some greaseproof paper on a tray or plate.

7. Cover a surface with icing sugar (for white truffles) or cocoa powder (for milk and dark). Using dusted hands, take spoonfuls of truffle mixture and shape it into balls. Place each ball on the greaseproof paper.

8. Return the truffles to the fridge.

9. Prepare the chocolate coating by following the recipe for your chosen chocolate. For white chocolate-coated truffles, you may prefer to omit the vanilla chip, to stop vanilla seeds blemishing the chocolate.

10. The chocolate is ready to use when it reaches the 'sticky' stage (see Chocolate Thickness Chart p.97). If your chocolate is too thin, allow it to cool a little before use.

11. Place some more greaseproof paper on another placemat, tray or plate.

12. Remove the truffles from the fridge and dip them in the chocolate, using either a fork or chocolate dipping tool.

13. Place each finished truffle on the greaseproof paper.

14. Decorate or ice the truffles (p.62).

15. When you have finished decorating the truffles, put them in the fridge so that the chocolate can set.

16. Store in the fridge for up to 5 days.

17. Remove from the fridge and either indulge yourself, or use them to wow guests.

For photo, see overleaf

ICING TRUFFLES

You can ice truffles using either melted chocolate or sugar icing.

If you want the icing to blend with the coating, ice the truffles before they set. If you're happy for the icing to sit atop the chocolate, you can decorate them whenever you like.

For chocolate, prepare a small quantity of your chosen kind. It's ready to use when it reaches the gloopy stage (see Chocolate Thickness Chart p.97). Prepare icing by combining icing sugar, water and, for chocolate icing, cocoa powder. The icing should be thick enough to hold its shape, but not too solid to push through a nozzle.

Fit a narrow nozzle to a piping bag. I prefer disposable piping bags, as the reusable ones tend to get spoilt pretty quickly.

Spoon the chocolate/icing into the piping bag.

Hover the piping bag near one of the chocolates, angled slightly upwards so the mixture doesn't run out until you want to use it.

Tilt the nozzle downwards and gently squeeze the bag until chocolate/icing comes out. For stripes, pipe a zigzag that extends slightly beyond the chocolate. Another impressive way to decorate a truffle is to draw a spiral on it.

If the chocolate/icing is too thin, you won't need to squeeze the bag as the mixture will flow of its own accord. In that case, you'll have to act fast, or it will go everywhere.

DECORATING TRUFFLES

Truffles look delicious covered in chopped nuts, desiccated coconut or hundreds and thousands. Toppings can also hide a multitude of sins, should your truffles not turn out quite as expected.

You should decorate truffles as quickly as you can, so that the chocolate is still sticky enough for the toppings to stick.

Make sure there is plenty of space between truffles that will have different toppings, pinch a little topping between your thumb and forefinger, and sprinkle over the chocolate-coated truffles.

FLAVOURING TRUFFLES

If you wish to flavour truffles, I recommend adding flavouring to the middle mixture and not the coating, so that you get a hit of flavour when you bite into the truffle. The truffle mixture behaves a little differently to chocolate, so you can use either flavoured oils or alcohol-based extracts.

Orange

Add a few drops of orange essence or orange liqueur, and 1 tsp grated orange zest.

Rum

Add a few drops of rum or rum essence.

Chilli

Add a few drops of chilli oil (made by leaving chopped chillies to soak in olive oil for 5 days).

Coffee

Add 1-2 tsps espresso powder.

Millionaire's Salted Caramel Cups

Chocolates inspired by desserts combine two of my favourite things, so I had to include a chocolate influenced by the caramel slice. Salted caramel is a very 'en vogue' flavour, but I'm not one to be steered by fashion – I picked it because it's delicious!

If you're short of time, you can easily omit the shortbread to make very satisfying caramel cups.

You will need one tray of individual, fillable moulds.

INGREDIENTS

100g milk chocolate (p.22)

100g shortbread (p.65)

2 tbsp caramelised sweetened condensed milk (p.85)

¼ tsp sea salt

✔ vegetarian

✔ nut free

! contains gluten

makes roughly 250g

(e.g. twenty 20 x 18mm fluted rounds)

METHOD

1. Make shortbread (p.65).

2. While it's cooking, prepare a batch of milk chocolate. It's ready to use once thin enough to spoon but still thick enough to stick to the sides of the moulds (the gloopy stage, p.97).

3. Little by little, spoon half of the chocolate into the moulds until each one is about one-third full. Use the handle of a teaspoon to spread the chocolate around the sides of each cavity. If the chocolate runs off the sides, put the moulds in the fridge for a couple of minutes and then retry spreading.

4. Once coated, place the part-filled moulds in the fridge to set. Leave the remaining molten chocolate over your pan of water. Stir occasionally but don't apply additional heat unless it starts to set.

5. To make the salted caramel, combine the caramelised condensed milk and sea salt. Mix well.

6. Spoon a little salted caramel into each chocolate cup, leaving enough room for the shortbread and a final layer of chocolate.

7. Place a shortbread medallion on top of the caramel in each chocolate. If the shortbread has spread, ending up too large for the moulds, crumble it on top of the caramel instead.

8. Pour just enough of the remaining chocolate into each mould to cover the caramel. If there is chocolate left afterwards, top up the moulds with the remainder.

9. Refrigerate for 1 hour then carefully press the chocolates out of the moulds.

10. Store in the fridge for up to 5 days.

For photo, see overleaf

Shortbread (For Millionaire's Salted Caramel Cups)

INGREDIENTS

25g cornflour

25g plain flour

10g caster sugar

30g butter, diced

✔ vegetarian

✔ nut free

! contains gluten

makes 100g

METHOD

1. Preheat the oven to 190°C.
2. Sieve the flour and cornflour into a bowl. Add the sugar and diced butter. Rub the fat into the flour using the tips of your fingers, until it forms a stiff dough.
3. Sprinkle some cornflour onto a clean, flat surface and knead the dough for a couple of minutes. Shape the dough into a sausage 2-3mm thinner in diameter than your chocolate moulds.
4. Cut 5mm medallions from the sausage and place on a baking tray lined with greaseproof paper. Put in the oven for 8 minutes.
5. This shortbread quantity errs on the side of caution, so it's likely you'll have some leftovers to nibble.

Oaty Biscuits (For Peanut Butter Cups)

INGREDIENTS

25g wholemeal plain flour

25g oats

10g soft brown sugar

30g butter, diced

✔ vegetarian

✔ nut free

! contains gluten

makes 100g

METHOD

1. Preheat the oven to 190°C.
2. Sieve the flour and oats into a bowl. Add the sugar and diced butter. Rub the fat into the flour using the tips of your fingers, until it forms a stiff dough.
3. Sprinkle some flour onto a clean, flat surface and knead the dough for a couple of minutes. Roll the dough until it is 4mm thick and cut into circles 4mm smaller in diameter than your moulds. For my cupcake cases, I used a 40mm cutter.
4. Place the circles on a baking tray lined with greaseproof paper. Put in the oven for 10 minutes.
5. This recipe makes 3-4 more biscuits than I need for my peanut butter cups but it's better to make a few extra in case the dimensions of your moulds call for more.

Peanut Butter Cups with Oaty Biscuit

Crunchy peanut butter encased in plain chocolate is an absolute treat. Oaty biscuit adds that little bit extra, to nudge this popular treat into gourmet territory. Having said that, if you're short on time, you can easily omit the biscuit. I use bun cases filled to 20mm, to give these a wide base, recreating the popular peanut cups you can buy commercially.

You will need silicone bun cases.

INGREDIENTS

200g plain chocolate (p.20)

100g oaty biscuits (p.65)

100g peanut butter (p.88)

✔ vegetarian

! contains nuts

! contains gluten

makes 300g

(e.g. 12 silicone cupcake cases)

METHOD

1. Make a batch of oaty biscuits (p.65).

2. While they're cooking, prepare a batch of plain chocolate. It's ready to use once it's thin enough to spoon, but still thick enough to stick to the sides of the moulds (i.e. the gloopy stage, p.97).

3. Little by little, spoon half of the chocolate into the cases until each one is about 15mm full. Use the handle of a teaspoon to spread the chocolate around the sides of each case, up to about 30mm. If the chocolate runs off the sides, put the moulds in the fridge for a couple of minutes and then retry spreading.

4. Once coated, place the cases in the fridge to set. Leave the remaining molten chocolate over your pan of water. Stir occasionally but don't apply additional heat unless it starts to set.

5. Prepare your peanut butter (p.88). You can use shop-bought peanut butter if you'd prefer.

6. Spoon a little peanut butter into each chocolate cup, leaving enough room for the biscuits and a final layer of chocolate.

7. Place a biscuit on top of the peanut butter in each case. If the biscuit is too large for the moulds because it has spread, break bits off. It doesn't matter if the biscuit is in crumbs; they'll still taste yummy.

8. Pour just enough of the remaining chocolate into each mould so that it covers the biscuits. If there is chocolate left afterwards, top up each case with the remainder.

9. Refrigerate for 1 hour.

10. Carefully press the chocolates out of the moulds.

11. Store in the fridge for up to 5 days.

Blackberry Fools

The beauty of blackberries is that, in season, you can pick them from hedgerows. They also have a magnificent flavour, like blackcurrants but with their own distinctive twist, reminiscent of autumn. Having a typically sharp tang, blackberries are traditionally used in jam and pies. However, adding a little clotted cream and a dash of sugar makes a scrumptious fruit fool. Fools are usually eaten like yoghurts, but also happen to make a wonderful filling for chocolate.

You will need one tray of individual, fillable moulds.

INGREDIENTS

100g white chocolate (p. 24)

50g Cornish clotted cream

100g blackberries

10g icing sugar

✔ vegetarian

✔ nut free

✔ gluten free

makes 200g

(e.g. sixteen 27 x 18mm rounds)

METHOD

1. Prepare a batch of white chocolate. It's ready to use once it's thin enough to spoon, but still thick enough to stick to the sides of the moulds (i.e. the gloopy stage, p.97).

2. Pour one half of the chocolate into deep moulds, until they're one-third full. Put in the fridge to set while you make the blackberry filling. Keep retrieving the chocolate from the fridge and tilting the mould so that the chocolate covers the sides. You might want to encourage it with the handle of a teaspoon. The cooler the chocolate, the more it will stick to the sides. Leave the remaining molten chocolate over your pan of water. Stir occasionally but don't apply additional heat unless it starts to set.

3. Blend the blackberries in an electric blender and place in a sieve over an empty bowl. This will remove those pesky seeds and leave a smooth juice.

4. Combine 4 tablespoons of the blackberry juice with the icing sugar and clotted cream.

5. Whisk until thick.

6. Remove the chocolate cups from the fridge. Using a teaspoon, carefully fill each chocolate to 2mm below the total depth of the mould.

7. Pour just enough of the remaining chocolate into each mould so that it covers the filling. If there is chocolate left afterwards, top up the moulds with the remainder.

8. Refrigerate for 1 hour.

9. Carefully press the chocolates out of the moulds.

10. Store in the fridge for up to 3 days, or until the best-before date of the clotted cream.

ALSO TRY

Raspberry fools, Gooseberry fools

Follow recipe above, substituting blackberries for other fruit.

Rhubarb fools

Cook the rhubarb then blend.

For photo, see p.53

Candied Orange Peel

It's surprisingly hard to buy candied orange peel, and when I do find it, it tends to be very expensive, given how quickly I can devour it. Fortunately, it can be made at home for a fraction of the price. And it's fruit, so you can pretend to yourself that it's healthy.

INGREDIENTS

100g plain (p.20) or milk chocolate (p.22)

the peel of 3 small oranges

2 tbsp honey

boiling water

✔ vegetarian

✔ nut free

✔ gluten free

makes 200g

(72 pieces)

METHOD

1. Cut an orange into 8 segments and use a knife to peel out the flesh.

2. Chop the remaining peel into slices, lengthwise.

3. Drop the slices into a pan of water and boil for 10 minutes with the lid on.

4. Drain the water.

5. Preheat your oven to 110°C.

6. Refill the pan with just enough boiling water to cover the orange. This time add honey to the water.

7. Boil without a lid until the liquid has reduced to a syrup.

8. Spread the strips on a baking sheet and place in the oven for 1 hour.

9. Meanwhile, prepare a batch of plain chocolate. It's ready to use once a teaspoon comes out with a thick but smooth coasting (i.e. the sticky stage, p.97).

10. Allow to cool.

11. Line a plate, tray or mat with greaseproof paper.

12. Grab each piece of peel by one end, and dip it in the chocolate. Place carefully on the greaseproof paper.

13. Transfer to the fridge for 1 hour.

14. Store in the fridge and eat within 5 days.

For photo please see overleaf

Dark Chocolate Gingers

My crystallised ginger recipe will blow your head off, and that's just the way I like it. Plain chocolate makes the perfect coating by giving you a sweet, rich, chocolate hit before the fire of the ginger hits your palate.

INGREDIENTS

100g plain chocolate (p.20)

300g ginger

3 tbsp honey

boiling water

✔ vegetarian

✔ nut free

✔ gluten free

makes 300g

(about 20 pieces)

METHOD

1. Peel the fresh ginger. You should end up with about 200g.

2. Cut into chunks. I make mine about 2-3cm big, but you may prefer smaller chunks for a more subtle ginger experience.

3. Put the ginger in a saucepan and cover with boiling water.

4. Boil gently for 45 minutes.

5. Drain the ginger.

6. Return the ginger to the pan and cover with boiling water once again.

7. Add honey to the water.

8. Allow to simmer for another 50 minutes. Keep checking the pan. If it looks as though it's about to run dry, add more boiling water.

9. Once the 50 minutes have passed, allow the liquid to boil off until you're left with a thick syrup.

10. Allow to cool.

11. Prepare a batch of plain chocolate. It's ready to use when it reaches the sticky stage (see Chocolate Thickness Chart p.97).

12. Remove the ginger chunks from the pan and allow to cool.

13. Line a tray, plate or mat with greaseproof paper.

14. Dip the ginger in the chocolate using either chocolate dipping tools or a pair of forks.

15. Place each piece of coated ginger carefully on the greaseproof paper.

16. Put the ginger chunks in the fridge for half an hour to set.

17. Store in the fridge and eat within 5 days.

More Recipe Variations

CRÈMES

Blueberry Bombs

- Prepare the blueberries as strawberries and pipe into spherical moulds for a quirky take on traditional fruit crèmes.

Orange Crème

- Make peppermint crèmes, but use orange oil instead of peppermint. You may also like to use a few drops of carrot juice (p.86) to colour.

Plain Fondant Centre

- Leave out the colours and flavouring, for a fresh and sugary chocolate bar filling for those with a sweet tooth.

CANDIED FRUITS

Lime

- Crystallise lime strips, as per candied orange, then chop them into small squares and scatter upon dark chocolate.

Lemon

- Crystallise lemon strips, as per candied orange, then cut into slivers and hide in a white chocolate mousse (p.54 but without the cocoa powder).

PRALINES

Hazelnut, Walnut, Pecans or Almonds

- Make as per pistachio pralines, but change the nut. Ground almonds are easier to come by than crushed versions of the others, so skip a step by buying your almonds ready-ground.

WAYS TO USE UP CONDENSED MILK

- Pour it over winter puddings such as crumble or steam pudding.
- Use it in a trifle instead of custard.
- Turn it into caramel. Follow instructions for caramel sauce (p.85) and keep heating until it reaches the consistency of fudge.

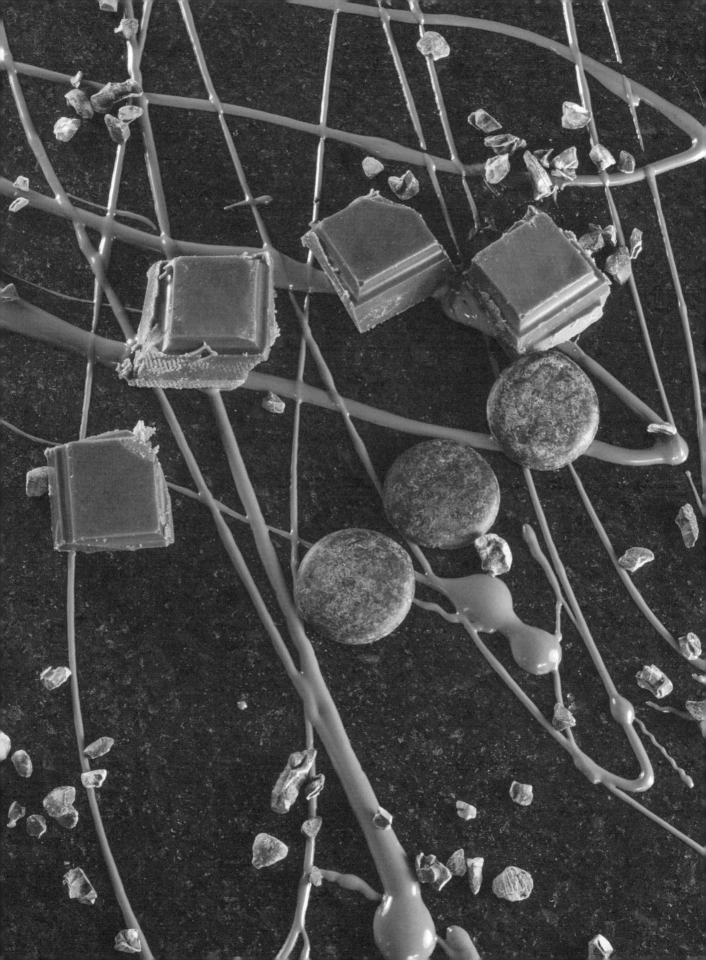

Seasonal and Novelty Chocolate

Most, if not *all,* of the festivals in my social calendar are celebrated with chocolate. So it would be negligent to write a chocolate recipe book that didn't cover, at the very least, Christmas and Easter.

I've also included ideas, such as modelling and structure building, to add that personal touch to birthdays and other special occasions.

I haven't included the recipe for chocolate letters (see opposite), as I've covered making and pouring chocolate in earlier sections. Look for letter moulds that are chunky, as it's tricky to get chocolate out of fiddly moulds without breaking it.

Right: fondant eggs, fondant models, chocolate letters

Christmas-Spiced Chocolate Treats

We associate many flavours with Christmas, for example spices like cinnamon, clove and star anise. Then there are fruits like orange and cherry.

With a range of seasonal moulds out there, Christmas-spiced chocolates make a lovely treat for guests, or can be boxed and given to people as presents.

Chocolate moulds tend to be small and fiddly so, rather than filling chocolates, I've developed a recipe where the Christmas flavourings blend in with the chocolate. Many novelty chocolate moulds have intricate details, so I recommend a chocolate that hasn't had much added to it, such as plain.

You will need two trays of Christmas-shaped moulds.

INGREDIENTS

100g plain chocolate (p.20)

½ tsp ground cinnamon

½ tsp ground ginger

up to 5 drops of orange oil

✔ vegan option

✔ nut free

✔ gluten free

makes roughly 105g

(e.g. 16 small chocolate shapes)

METHOD

1. Make a batch of chocolate but when you add the sweetener, also add cinnamon and ginger. Add the orange oil, drop by drop. Taste the chocolate; if the flavour is too subtle, add more of the oil. Be careful not to add too much, or the chocolate might not set.

2. Continue making the chocolate as per your chosen recipe. The chocolate is ready to use as soon as it pours smoothly during the second heating stage.

3. If the moulds are floppy, put them on placemats for easy lifting. Carefully pour the chocolate into the moulds.

4. Immediately transfer the moulds to the fridge.

5. Refrigerate for 1 hour.

6. Remove the moulds from the fridge and pop out the chocolate very carefully, paying particular attention to any fiddly details, such as antlers and candy canes.

7. Store in the fridge for up to 5 days.

Chocolate Block Building

Building with chocolate blocks is a great novelty activity, which you can do either for fun or as a special treat for a loved one.

Building With Chocolate Bricks

You will need two trays of brick moulds.

INGREDIENTS

200g chocolate of your choice

METHOD

1. Prepare a double batch of chocolate from section 1. Pour it into brick moulds.
2. Let the chocolate set for 2 hours. If the chocolate's not completely solid, the bumps tend to stay in the mould when you try to press out the bricks.
3. Fill a mug with boiling water.
4. To stick one brick on the top of another:
    a. Dip a palette knife in the water for a few seconds, to heat it. Dry with kitchen roll.
    b. Run the hot palette knife over the top of the lower brick until the bumps melt.
    c. Press the next brick on top of the first, using the molten chocolate to stick them together.
5. Repeat until you've created the model of your dreams.
6. Store in the fridge for up to 5 days. (The chocolate surface may discolour with time.)

Fondant People

You will need one tray of people moulds.

INGREDIENTS

230g fondant in various colours (p.79)

METHOD

1. Make coloured fondant icing as per Chocolate Fondant Models (p.79). Knead well.
2. Lightly dust chocolate moulds in cornflour.
3. For the heads, make blobs out of yellow fondant, and gently squeeze them into place in the moulds.
4. Next do the hands.
5. Now make blobs out of contrasting colours. Press these into place for the torso.
6. Repeat for the legs.
7. Allow to dry overnight.
8. Attempt to take one out. If it crumbles, put the mould in the freezer for 20 minutes and try again.

Fondant Eggs

Chocolate shells filled with fondant have been popular for decades. However, they have one fatal drawback – they are a seasonal food. Every January, I wait expectantly for the first Easter eggs to come out. However, fondant eggs are much easier to make than you might imagine.

You will need one tray of fillable egg moulds.

INGREDIENTS

100g milk chocolate

For the egg white

60g fondant icing sugar

a few drops of water

For the egg yolk

30g fondant icing sugar

1 tsp puréed mango

1 drop of orange flavouring (optional)

3 drops yellow food colouring (optional)

✔ vegetarian

✔ nut free

✔ gluten free

makes 150g

(e.g. ten 32 x 45 x 17mm eggs)

METHOD

1. Prepare a batch of chocolate of your choice. It's ready to use once it reaches the gloopy stage (see Chocolate Thickness Chart p.97).

2. Spoon the chocolate into egg moulds, making sure that every side is covered in at least 2mm of chocolate and that you leave a large enough cavity for the fondant.

3. Put the chocolate shells in the fridge for 10 minutes.

4. Meanwhile, prepare the fondant.

    a. White fondant: add water to 60g fondant icing sugar, one drop at a time, until it's reached the perfect consistency – gloopy but not runny.

    b. Yellow fondant: cut up a mango. Purée a few slices using a mini-chopper or a fork. Little by little, add puréed mango to 30g fondant icing sugar, until it reaches the consistency of the white fondant. You may like to add a drop of orange flavouring. For a deeper yellow, add a few drops of yellow food colouring.

5. Remove the moulds from the fridge.

6. Spoon white fondant into the moulds, spreading it around so that it touches all the sides.

7. Spoon a little yellow fondant (the yoke) into the centre of each mould. Level off with a palette knife.

8. Put the moulds in the freezer for half an hour. This will solidify the fondant, making the eggs easier to press out of the moulds without breaking.

9. Remove the eggs from the freezer and carefully press the halves out of the mould.

10. Heat a palette knife by dipping the end in boiling water and wiping it dry. Use the palette knife to smooth off two egg halves, until each has a flat surface. Push them together and hold for a few seconds so that the melted chocolate can fuse together.

11. Repeat for the remaining egg halves.

12. Store in the fridge for up to 4 days.

For photo see p.75

Chocolate Fondant Models

Although not strictly chocolate, because it contains no cocoa butter, fondant can be flavoured with cocoa powder and then used to model cake decorations and novelty sweets. The easiest way to make fondant is to use fondant icing sugar and water.

INGREDIENTS

100g fondant icing sugar

15g cocoa powder (optional)

food colouring (optional) (p.86)

5-6 tsp water

✔ vegetarian

✔ nut free

✔ gluten free

makes 115g

METHOD

1. Sift the icing sugar into a bowl.
2. For chocolate, add cocoa powder. For coloured, add a few drops of food colouring, or follow the steps on page 86 concerning icing.
3. Add the water little by little while stirring, until it starts to resemble modelling clay. If it gets too wet, you can recue it by adding more icing sugar.
4. Knead the mixture until it's smooth and easy to work with.
5. Store in a cool dry place, indefinitely.

GINGERBREAD CHARACTERS

You will need a mini-gingerbread-person cutter.

Roll chocolate fondant until it's 3mm thick. Using a cutter, cut gingerbread character shapes.

Take a little white fondant. Roll it into tiny balls for the eyes and buttons. Create a minuscule sausage and curve it to form the mouth. If you have difficulty getting the details to stick to the characters, dip the end of a skewer or fine paintbrush in water and use the water like glue.

ANIMALS

Grab a blob of chocolate icing and roll it into a ball. Repeat.

Stick the balls together using a paintbrush and a dab of water.

Make a pair of legs or arms by rolling a sausage and cutting it diagonally.

Make ears by rolling into balls or sausages, and squishing them. You may wish to use blobs of another colour to line ears.

Make a nose with a tiny blob.

Draw on eyes and other details using a fine paintbrush dipped in black food colouring.

For photo see p.75

The Chocolate Cupboard

There are some ingredients that crop up over and over in this recipe book, so I decided to give them their own section.

Not all cocoa extracts can be made at home with regular kitchen equipment but making those that can allows you to delve deep into the chocolate-making process – a real treat for enthusiasts.

Nut butter is very simple to make. It can be easier to make your own than find somewhere that sells it, especially in the case of cashew butter, which isn't as readily available as its peanut cousin.

You will also find non-food related information, such as how to make silicone moulds and presentation boxes. Making your own moulds is enormous fun, and an activity that I highly recommend.

Right: presentation boxes, coloured chocolate, cocoa nibs, peanut butter.

Roasted Cocoa Nibs

Many supermarkets now stock cocoa nibs, but it can be very satisfying, not to mention flavoursome, to prepare your own using raw cocoa beans. Separating shells and nibs does require patience but we're dealing with very small quantities, so I think you'll find it worthwhile.

INGREDIENTS

120g cocoa beans   Makes 100g

METHOD

1. Heat the oven to 110°C.

2. Spread the cocoa beans on a baking tray.

3. Roast for 30 minutes.

4. Allow to cool until they're cold enough to handle. It's slightly easier to separate the shells if the beans are still warm, as the nibs are more likely to stay fused together.

5. Separate the shells and nibs using your fingers. If any beans are particularly tough to get into, press down on the bean using the side of a knife. Discard the tough casing.

For photo, see page 83.

Cocoa Liquor

Cocoa liquor, also known as cocoa paste, is available from most cocoa butter stockists. However, for the ultimate flavour, you can make your own using nibs from cocoa beans. It's a slow process and requires much patience, so only try this if you're really keen to delve deep into the process of chocolate preparation.

Although solid at room temperature, the friction from grinding the nibs causes heat that gives cocoa liquor a paste-like texture. When heated, it melts beautifully.

INGREDIENTS

100g roasted cocoa nibs (see above)   Makes 100g

METHOD

1. Preheat the oven to 110°C.

2. Spread the cocoa nibs out on a baking tray and toast for 30 minutes.

3. Allow to cool slightly.

4. Put the roasted nibs in a small, electric chopper or grinder and blitz until they form a smooth paste. This may take up to 10 minutes so check the instructions on your blender. You may need to do it in smaller stints to stop the blender overheating.

5. Use as directed by your recipe (e.g. ultimate chocolate p.26) or substitute cocoa powder with cocoa liquor in any other chocolate – I recommend adding a little at a time until you reach your required flavour.

Vanilla Chips

If your recipe calls for vanilla chips, you can use ½ tsp vanilla seeds or additive-free paste instead. Vanilla chips are simply a way of storing vanilla seeds.

Adding vanilla essence to chocolate is hit and miss. Sometimes it combines perfectly and at other times is causes the mixture to seize, because most vanilla essence uses water to carry the vanilla.

For chocolate makers, the best carrier for vanilla is cocoa butter. Storing vanilla for future use is particularly handy because every pod contains far too many seeds for one batch of chocolate. Vanilla chips can go in the cupboard and be brought out whenever you need a hit of vanilla.

You will need individual moulds.

INGREDIENTS

1 vanilla pod

5g cocoa butter   makes 8

METHOD

1. Melt the cocoa butter in a bowl above boiling water.
2. Cut the vanilla pod lengthwise and scrape out the vanilla seeds with a sharp knife.
3. Add the vanilla seeds to the melted cocoa butter and stir well.
4. Allow to cool slightly then stir.
5. Pour into 8 individual moulds.
6. Use as directed by your recipe. These are not for nibbling on!

Caramelised Condensed Milk

Some sweetened condensed milk manufacturers also sell a caramelised variety, but it's harder to come by than the original kind. Turning condensed milk into caramel is incredibly easy.

Many people make caramel sauce by placing the unopened can in a pan of hot water. However, cans have been known to explode. So, in the interest of not blowing up your kitchen, try heating the condensed milk in a bowl above boiling water.

INGREDIENTS

the same weight of condensed milk as you will need in caramel

METHOD

1. Pour a can of sweetened, condensed milk into a heatproof bowl or melting pot above a pan of boiling water. Unlike chocolate making, it's best if the bowl does touch the water.
2. Place on a low heat and simmer, stirring occasionally until the milk turns golden, usually 1-2 hours.
3. Whip the mixture to ensure an even texture.

Food Colourings

Artificial food colourings have been under attack for decades. Many people believe they lead to hyperactivity in children, and some dyes have been linked to cancer.

Do you need to avoid them? It's up to you. But you certainly don't need to have them.

It can be hard to create vivid colours using natural dyes, but I personally find luminescent colours extremely off-putting in confectionary.

The best thing about natural dyes is that you can make them at home extremely easily. Below are my tips on getting some of the classic colours.

Because you sometimes need so much of a natural dye to colour chocolate, the colouring can stop it from setting – there are just too many added ingredients. Therefore I recommend keeping the chocolate its natural shade and using a tiny bit of pure cocoa butter mixed with food colouring to add a flash of colour (p.40).

Red

Both strawberry purée and beetroot juice make satisfying deep pinks. You can taste the flavours but neither is unpleasant – beetroot makes a surprisingly tasty icing.

To collect beetroot juice, blend cooked beetroot and then sieve it. Shop-bought cooked beetroot often comes in its own juices, which you can use as well.

For chocolate, colour cocoa butter with a few drops of beetroot juice, as strawberry purée will mess up the texture.

For icing, use strawberry purée instead of water. To make strawberry purée, blend and then sieve to extract the seeds.

Yellow

By far the brightest way to make yellow is to use turmeric. A little goes a long way and you can make a vibrant yellow using a very small quantity. However, you *can* taste it, and it's nowhere near as charming as the taste of other foods used in colouring.

Another method is to use concentrated carrot juice. The juice may look orange but chocolate coloured with carrot juice sets yellow. Wash and scrape a carrot. There's no need to peel it unless it's particularly dirty. Cut the carrot into small pieces then blitz it in a blender. Add water, little by little, until it's smooth. Strain the carrot juice using a cheese cloth.

For chocolate, colour cocoa butter with a small quantity of ground turmeric or concentrated carrot juice.

For icing, add a small quantity of carrot juice to icing sugar.

If you're happier with a paler yellow, then mango makes a delicious lemon-coloured icing. Simply pulp the flesh of the mango until smooth, and add it to icing sugar, instead of water.

Green

I colour my foods green with blended, boiled spinach. It may sound disgusting to some but the taste is barely present in foods.

Make the colouring by boiling the spinach until there's only a little liquid left. Tip the contents of the pan into a small blender and blend until smooth. Collect the liquid by straining the blended spinach through a cheese cloth.

For chocolate, colour cocoa butter with a few drops of the spinach dye.

For icing, use the spinach liquid instead of water.

Blue

Making blue is fun because it feels like a particularly enjoyable school science experiment. It's made from red cabbage and bicarbonate of soda.

Chop up one third of a large red cabbage. Boil for about half an hour. The water will turn purple. Reduce until there are only a few drops left.

Strain the remaining liquid into a bowl. Using a cocktail stick, grab a tiny amount of bicarbonate of soda. Add it to the liquid and stir. The liquid should start to change colour. Bear in mind that if you add too much, the mixture will go turquoise and then green. More importantly, use bicarb sparingly because it tastes horrible.

For chocolate, colour cocoa butter with a few drops of red cabbage dye.

For icing, using the dye instead of water.

STORAGE

Prepare dyes as and when you need them, and use the same day.

TIP FOR CREATING RICHER COLOURS

For wet dyes, the more food you use, and the more you reduce the liquid, the more concentrated the dye will be. Boil the liquid until it shrinks to the quantity that you require then use all of it.

For photo, see p.83.

Peanut Butter

INGREDIENTS

95g roasted peanuts

2 tsp caster sugar

splash of olive oil

makes 100g

METHOD

- Put all the ingredients in a blender.
- Blitz until smooth.
- Use as directed by your recipe.
- Can be stored in the fridge for up to a week.

For photo, see page 83.

Cashew Butter

INGREDIENTS

cashew nuts

METHOD

1. Weigh the same amount of raw cashew nuts as your recipe needs in cashew butter.
2. Blitz in a blender until smooth.
3. Use as directed by your recipe.
4. Can be stored in the fridge for up to a week.

Presentation Boxes

box width

box height

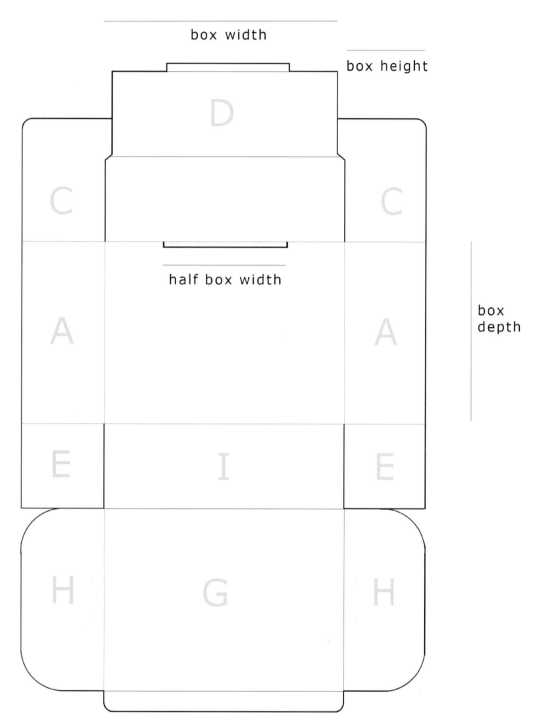

D

C

C

half box width

box depth

A

A

E

I

E

H

G

H

Decide on your dimensions then copy this net onto cardboard using a pen, ruler and set square.
Cut along the thick lines. Score the thin lines with a penknife or the blade of the scissors.
Fold sides A and B towards you. Fold in wings C so that their tabs tuck into the hole. Fold over wall D, to create your first side. Fold wings E inward. Fold sides H, I and lid G inwards. Tuck in the final tab.

For photo, see page 83.

Silicone Moulds

You can buy many different kinds of chocolate mould, but sometimes you'll find your heart set on something you simply cannot find. Don't give up. Silicone moulds are cheap and simple to make.

YOU WILL NEED

200g culinary grade silicone putty

50g oven-hardening modelling clay (optional)

METHOD

1. a) Find something you would like to copy, such as a coin or building brick.

   or

   b) Make an item using oven-hardening modelling clay such as Fimo. This works like Plasticine but with the additional feature that it will harden when baked.

   Create a figure or prop, the size and shape of the chocolate you would like to cast.

   Avoid thin features such as tails and antlers, or the chocolate might break when removed from the moulds.

   Remember that only one side of your model will be moulded, and that the model will need to press cleanly against the silicone and release easily.

   Bake the modelling clay in the oven in accordance with its instructions.

2. Silicone putty comes as two substances that need to be combined to activate. Knead these together. Once the putty is a consistent colour, it's ready to use. You'll have a limited time before it starts to set, so work quickly.

3. Take a little putty and use your fingers to press it around details on the side of the figure that you wish to cast.

4. Roll the rest of the putty to twice the thickness of the item you're casting.

5. Press the item into the putty.

6. Leave to cure for 2 hours at room temperature, or as directed by the manufacturer.

7. Separate your model from your silicone.

8. Use the silicone mould as you would a shop-bought mould.

APPENDIX 1

Troubleshooting

Chocolate mixture is too sweet

If you're making milk or plain chocolate, try adding a little extra cocoa powder to balance out the sweetness. If this doesn't work, you'll need to add more cocoa butter.

To add cocoa butter, first return the mixture to the heat. If you break up / grate the new cocoa butter first, it'll dissolve quicker and prevent you from needing to heat the chocolate much. Add about 10g of cocoa butter to the mixture. Keep stirring, so that the cocoa butter combines using the minimum heat necessary. *Then* follow the steps for working chocolate on a slab. If you've already worked the chocolate on your slab, you will need to do it again.

Chocolate mixture tastes too much like cocoa

First try adding a little more sweetener. If the cocoa is still overpowering the other flavours, you will need to add more fat, either cocoa or coconut butter.

Coconut butter melts at a lower temperature than cocoa powder. If your mixture is still fairly warm, you can avoid reheating it by using coconut butter instead of cocoa. Stir in 10g.

If you'd rather add cocoa butter, follow the paragraph 'To add cocoa butter...' from the section above.

Milk chocolate tastes like plain chocolate

This is usually because you have used too much cocoa powder. Cocoa powder can overpower other flavours. More than 1 tablespoon of cocoa powder for every 50g of cocoa butter will create a very dark flavour.

You could try adding more powdered or condensed milk, but be careful when increasing the milk content, as it can affect the consistency of the chocolate. Make sure that you use *full cream* milk powder, as skimmed will not add the necessary creaminess.

Another option is to use deodorised cocoa butter instead of regular. It's had its flavour removed and therefore allows milk to dominate.

Powdered milk won't dissolve into condensed milk

If you can't get powdered milk to dissolve into sweetened condensed milk, the easiest thing to do is to leave it out. Condensed milk has a strong enough flavour to add creaminess to chocolate, with or without that extra spoonful of powdered milk.

However, if you're determined to include powdered milk, then you have two choices. Either use *instant* milk powder instead of powdered milk; this contains the additive lecithin, which will help the ingredients combine. Or, blitz your powdered milk in a grinder until it reaches the consistency of flour, and then stir it into your condensed milk. Make sure that you're using *full cream* milk powder, not skimmed.

Chocolate mixture is too thick

Heating the chocolate should thin it out. Make sure that no moisture gets into the mixture.

If the mixture still won't thin, check that you've used the correct proportions of ingredients. Too much sweetener or milk products makes a mixture overly thick.

Chocolate mixture is too thin

Cooling the mixture will help thicken it. The best way to cool it is on a slab.

Being careful to wipe any condensation off the bottom of the bowl, pour the mixture onto a slab, using a scraper and/or palette knife to ensure that it doesn't run off the edges.

Cool the mixture by working it back and forth with the scraper. Repeatedly spread it out to increase the surface area then scrape it back together. If the mixture doesn't start to thicken after 5 minutes, try opening a window to cool down your kitchen.

Once the mixture reaches the consistency of margarine, scrape it back into the bowl and return it to the pan, stirring continuously.

Gently re-heat the chocolate until it is just thin enough to use.

Chocolate mixture has turned to the consistency of treacle

If, despite applying heat, your mixture won't thin no matter how hard you try, and has turned to the consistency of thick treacle, then it has probably 'seized'.

This usually means that some water has got into the chocolate mixture. This could be something as simple as a tiny drop dripping from a utensil, or it could be caused by using an ingredient that has attracted moisture from the air, such as old honey.

It is sometimes possible to rescue chocolate that has begun to separate on the heat. You could try pouring the contents onto a slab and working it until smooth. Then return it to a very gentle heat.

If you still can't rescue the mixture, you *can* turn it into something else. Slowly whisking in cream will make a tasty ganache.

Chocolate doesn't thicken / combine on slab

If you've been trying to work chocolate on a slab for over 10 minutes, and it's still showing no signs of coming together, then your work space is too hot.

The easiest thing to do is open a window or move your slab closer to an open window. If you've already tried that, scrape the chocolate back into the melting bowl and put it in the fridge for 3 minutes, then return the mixture to the slab.

Never wash your slab in warm water just before use. You want it to be as cool as possible. Run it under a cold tap, if you need to (but make sure you dry it thoroughly before it comes into contact with chocolate).

If you're using a makeshift slab, such as a tray, consider putting it in the fridge for a few minutes before use, as it won't be as naturally cool as granite/marble. If the tray is small, try working half of the chocolate first, then the other.

A trick for future chocolate making is not to let the mixture get too hot prior to working it on the slab. Take the cocoa butter off the heat as soon as it's completely dissolves. Make sure the cocoa butter is off the heat before adding the remaining ingredients.

Chocolate feels gritty on the tongue

There are two causes of gritty chocolate:

- The milk powder was not fine enough. Most commercially available milk powders are too coarse for making homemade chocolate. To make the milk powder finer, put it in a coffee grinder and whizz it until it reaches the texture of flour. Alternatively, you could replace the honey and milk powder with sweetened condensed milk.
- The cocoa liquor was not fine enough. If you've made your own liquor from nibs, you probably found that the grinding stage was frustratingly long. If you stop too soon, you do find that some grains crunch between your teeth in the finished chocolate. To prevent this in future chocolate, grind the nibs for longer.

Finished chocolate is too soft

If chocolate is soft after a long stretch in the fridge, then perhaps the proportion of cocoa butter to other ingredients was too low. It's the cocoa butter that helps chocolate to set, so if you add too much milk, sweeteners or flavourings, the resulting chocolate will be less solid than you might otherwise expect.

Another reason could be that the chocolate wasn't correctly thickened. Even though it sounds counter-intuitive, the process of cooling chocolate on a slab and then reheating it is crucial to the finished texture, as it controls the structure of crystals within the chocolate.

One solution is the give the chocolate to your friends and tell them it is fudge.

Chocolate separates out in the mould

This usually happens when:

- the cocoa butter didn't get hot enough when you melted it
- you have not worked your chocolate on a slab for long enough
- you let the chocolate get too thin during the reheating stage
- you didn't put it in the fridge immediately after pouring.

In the future, you could try using a thermometer to check that the mixture reaches key temperatures. When melting cocoa butter, it must reach 45°C. It then should cool to the margarine stage (see Chocolate Thickness Chart on page 97 for temperatures, which vary from chocolate to chocolate). Finally, raise the temperature again, until the temperature reaches at least the gloopy stage.

To rescue separated chocolate, pop it out of the mould and back into a melting pot until it melts. Refer back to your original recipe, and follow the steps for working the chocolate on a slab. Then return it to a gentle heat and stir until it reaches your required thickness.

Alternatively, you could experiment with powdered soy lecithin, an additive that helps combine ingredients. Be aware that you need to use lecithin sparingly.

There are gaps on top of moulded chocolate

There are two causes or chocolate not filling moulds perfectly:

- - The moulds were wet.
- - The chocolate was too sticky.

If my recipe calls for gloopy chocolate (usually used when you're lining moulds to be filled), you may find that the chocolate doesn't fill minute details on the top of the moulds. One way around this is to raise the temperature of your molten chocolate until it's thin enough to pour, and pour a fine layer into the moulds. Then let the chocolate cool to the gloopy stage, and finish lining the moulds.

Recipe yielded less chocolate than expected

The final weights given on each recipe are estimates. Many of my recipes allow you to vary proportions of sweetener and milk, thus there will be much individual variation in the finished weights of mixtures.

If you've used the maximum of each ingredient, and are still finding your finished weights fall short of expectations, stop 'sampling' so much along the way!

Silicone moulds are fiddly to clean

First wash in usual washing-up solution. Then rinse in boiling water. Give the moulds a good shake then leave somewhere draughty to dry.

Silicone moulds are difficult to dry

If you follow the above steps for washing your moulds, the boiling water should evaporate quickly.

If you need to dry moulds more rapidly, use either a *microfibre* cloth or a hair dryer. Regular tea towels and kitchen roll can leave fibres on the mould, which downgrade the appearance of the chocolate.

APPENDIX 2

Tempering Chocolate

People who work with chocolate will tell you that tempering is crucial if you want chocolate that sets quickly, doesn't melt in the hand, has a glossy surface and makes a satisfying snap when broken.

When chocolate is tempered, it's melted until the temperature reaches a certain maximum, then cooled rapidly, only to be raised in temperature once again. This ensures that only one type of crystal can form/remain during the cooling process.

There are many ways to temper chocolate, with many professional chefs using a slab-scraper technique, similar to the method we use to make sure that the ingredients combine in a way that prevents them from separating out in the moulds.

Melting cocoa butter is an essential step in making homemade chocolate, so we already mimic the tempering process when we follow a recipe.

- Melting the cocoa butter raises it to the first temperature required.
- Adding the other ingredients naturally lowers the temperature. Working the mixture on a slab until it reaches the consistency of margarine reduces it further.
- Gently reheating the chocolate to the consistency desirable for dipping/pouring brings it up to the final necessary temperature.

Different kinds of chocolate require different temperatures when tempering. However, temperature charts vary enormously from source to source, and our homemade chocolate differs from bought chocolate. Indeed, our chocolate varies from reader to reader, as you buy different varieties of ingredients and change proportions to match your personal taste.

Additionally, most kitchen thermometers take a while (10-20 seconds) to catch up, by which time, ideal temperatures have often passed. Even my dedicated, digital chocolate thermometer is slow.

Thus, I find it much easier to observe the chocolate's consistency than to fiddle around with a thermometer, especially when dealing with such small quantities of chocolate.

Generally, you'll make chocolate and use it right away, but if not, you'll need to temper it.

First, raise the temperature until the chocolate has melted to a smooth, thin consistency that you could pour easily. Plain will get thinner than white or milk.

Next, work the chocolate on a slab until it reaches the consistency of margarine.

Finally, return to the heat until it's thin enough for your needs.

High quality shop-bought chocolate will come with its own tempering instructions.

APPENDIX 3

Chocolate Thickness Chart

Appearance / Texture	Temperature (°C) *	Uses	Examples
Solid (hard)	Plain: under 22 Milk: under 22 White: under 22	Eating!	All finished chocolate.
Solid (soft) Chocolate is soft enough to stir, but too thick to work with and too sloppy to eat.	Plain: 22 - 26 Milk: 22 - 27 White: 22 - 27	Can be heated to make a useful consistency.	Often reached mid-recipe, after taking chocolate off slab.
Gloopy Sticks to a spatula in clumps.	Plain: 26 - 28 Milk: 27 - 29 White: 27 - 28	Lining moulds for fillings.	Strawberry hearts, blackberry fools, fondant eggs.
Sticky Thick but smooth. Sticks to spatula leaving a smooth finish.	Plain: 28 - 29 Milk: 29 - 30.5 White: 28 - 30	Coating.	Truffles, chocolate-coated ginger, chocolate-coated orange peel.
Pourable Smooth. Thin enough to pour. Runs off a spatula.	Plain: 29 - 31 Milk: 30.5 - 32 White: 30 - 32	Filling moulds.	Chocolate bars, Christmas-spiced chocolate treats.
Too hot Plain chocolate turns into a very thin liquid at high temperatures. Chocolate containing milk can become uneven as the cocoa butter and milk start to separate.	Plain: over 31 Milk: over 32 White: over 32	You can use this to fill moulds, but the ingredients may separate out. Consider cooling a little before use. You may need to redo the slab stage.	

* These temperatures are guidelines only. Critical temperatures vary depending on the proportions and brand of ingredients used. Thermometers vary and can take a while to reach temperature.

APPENDIX 4

Conversion Chart

Agave Nectar

1 teaspoon	6 grams	0.2 ounces
1 tablespoon	18 grams	0.6 ounces
5.6 tablespoons	**100 grams**	3.5 ounces
1.6 tablespoons	28 grams	**1 ounce**

Cashew Butter

1 teaspoon	6.7 grams	0.2 ounces
1 tablespoon	20 grams	0.7 ounces
5 tablespoons	**100 grams**	3.5 ounces
1.4 tablespoons	28 grams	**1 ounce**

Caster Sugar

1 teaspoon	4.7 grams	0.2 ounces
1 tablespoon	14 grams	0.5 ounces
7.1 tablespoons	**100 grams**	3.5 ounces
2 tablespoons	28 grams	**1 ounce**

Cocoa Butter

1 teaspoon	4 grams	0.1 ounces
1 tablespoon	12 grams	0.4 ounces
8.3 tablespoons	**100 grams**	3.5 ounces
2.4 tablespoons	28 grams	**1 ounce**

Cocoa Liquor

1 teaspoon	6 grams	0.2 ounces
1 tablespoon	18 grams	0.6 ounces
5.6 tablespoons	**100 grams**	3.5 ounces
1.6 tablespoons	28 grams	**1 ounce**

Cocoa Nibs

1 teaspoon	3.3 grams	0.1 ounces
1 tablespoon	10 grams	0.4 ounces
10 tablespoons	**100 grams**	3.5 ounces
2.8 tablespoons	28 grams	**1 ounce**

Cocoa Powder

1 teaspoon	2.3 grams	0.1 ounces
1 tablespoon	7 grams	0.2 ounces
14.3 tablespoons	**100 grams**	3.5 ounces
4 tablespoons	28 grams	**1 ounce**

Coconut Butter

1 teaspoon	2.7 grams	0.1 ounces
1 tablespoon	8 grams	0.3 ounces
12.5 tablespoons	**100 grams**	3.5 ounces
3.5 tablespoons	28 grams	**1 ounce**

Date Nectar

1 teaspoon	5.7 grams	0.2 ounces
1 tablespoon	17 grams	0.6 ounces
5.9 tablespoons	**100 grams**	3.5 ounces
1.7 tablespoons	28 grams	**1 ounce**

Honey

1 teaspoon	7.3 grams	0.3 ounces
1 tablespoon	22 grams	0.8 ounces
4.5 tablespoons	**100 grams**	3.5 ounces
1.3 tablespoons	28 grams	**1 ounce**

Icing Sugar

1 teaspoon	3.7 grams	0.1 ounces
1 tablespoon	11 grams	0.4 ounces
9.1 tablespoons	**100 grams**	3.5 ounces
2.6 tablespoons	28 grams	**1 ounce**

Powdered Milk

1 teaspoon	2.3 grams	0.1 ounces
1 tablespoon	7 grams	0.2 ounces
14.3 tablespoons	**100 grams**	3.5 ounces
4 tablespoons	28 grams	**1 ounce**

Sweetened Condensed Milk

1 teaspoon	7.7 grams	0.3 ounces
1 tablespoon	**23 grams**	0.8 ounces
4.3 tablespoons	100 grams	**3.5 ounces**
1.2 tablespoons	28 grams	1 ounce

Vanilla Chips

1 teaspoon	4 grams	0.1 ounces
1 tablespoon	12 grams	0.4 ounces
8.3 tablespoons	**100 grams**	3.5 ounces
2.4 tablespoons	28 grams	**1 ounce**

About Rosen Trevithick

Rosen is a chocolate enthusiast and bestselling author, who decided to combine her two passions to create a chocolate cookbook. She's a hobbyist rather than a chef, meaning that every recipe has been meticulously developed in her own kitchen, driven by a love of the craft.

Born in Cornwall and raised on Restronguet Creek, Rosen studied Psychology at St Catherine's College, Oxford, before moving back to the West Country. She now lives in Falmouth with two imaginary cats, fantasising about getting a real one.

Rosen has a variety of books in print including *My Granny Writes Erotica*, *Pompomberry House* and *The Troll Trap*, as well as over twenty digital titles.

She loves wild swimming, quiffs and vintage dresses. She dislikes house spiders, seagulls making a racket, and doing laundry.

RosenTrevithick.co.uk | facebook.com/rosentrevithick | twitter.com/rosentrevithick

Also by Rosen Trevithick

Novels

Pompomberry House | My Granny Writes Erotica - Threesome
Two Shades of the Lilac Sunset | Straight Out of University

Collections

Seesaw Volume I | Seesaw Volume II

Short Stories

The Other Daughter | London, the Doggy and Me | Lipstick and Knickers
The Selfish Act | On the Rocks | A Royal Mess | No Shades of Grey | The Ice Marathon

Non-Fiction

How Not to Self-Publish

Children's Books

My Babysitter is a Troll | The Troll Trap
Mr Splendiferous and the Troublesome Trolls
Trolls on Ice | Gourmet Girl Burger | The First Trollogy

  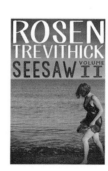 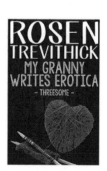 

About Claire Wilson

Claire Wilson is a professional photographer with a passion for food.

Claire has been a photographer for over 15 years. She produced photographs for Cornwall Today during 2009-2011, and for the walk book 'Discover Cornwall' by writer Sue Kittow. Claire is now focusing her energy on food photography and has enjoyed every moment learning how to make food look delicious.

As well as photography, Claire is an enthusiastic walker and cyclist, and enjoys exploring the Cornish coast. She lives in Penryn, Cornwall.

lle-photography.co.uk | facebook.com/llephotographycornwall

Photography by Claire Wilson

LLE Photography

Corporate Photography

Events Photography

Pet Photography

Landscapes

Claire also does fine art, food and product photography.